COMMUNITY ACTION

Working Partnerships
Community Development in Local Authorities

Maurice Broady was Professor of Social Policy, University College, Swansea from 1970 till 1982. The author of *Planning for People* and other books and articles on social planning and community development, he has been president of the National Federation of Community Organisations from 1977 till 1988, and chairman of the National Coalition for Neighbourhoods since 1984.

Rodney Hedley has been research and information officer at ADVANCE, the Greater London voluntary organisation for volunteering and neighbourhood development, since 1982. He is author of the evaluation guide for voluntary groups, *Measuring Success*, as well as a number of studies on neighbourhood care. Before working at ADVANCE, Rodney Hedley was research officer at the Centre for Policy on Ageing, following a career as a social worker. He is currently involved in research into volunteering and the black community.

Working Partnerships

Community Development in Local Authorities

Maurice Broady
&
Rodney Hedley

Illustrations by David Austin

Published in association with the
National Coalition for Neighbourhoods
by
Bedford Square Press

Published by
Bedford Square Press of the
National Council for Voluntary Organisations
26 Bedford Square, London WC1B 3HU

First published 1989

Typeset by The Wordshop
Printed and bound in England by J.W. Arrowsmith Ltd, Bristol

British Library Cataloguing in Publication Data

Broady, Maurice
Hedley, Rodney
  Community Partnerships
  Community Development in Local Authorities
  (Community action).
  1. Great Britain. Community work with
  ethnic minorities
  I. Title II. Series
  302.8.4.00941

ISBN 0–7199–1243–1

Contents

Dedication

The National Coalition would like to dedicate this book to
PADDY REINOLD,
the General Secretary of the National Federation of Community
Organisations from 1959 till 1982 and first joint secretary of the
Coalition. In so many ways, it is the outcome of his work for the
community movement over so many years.

Acknowledgements

I wish, as chairman of the National Coalition, to place on record the Coalition's appreciation of the many important contributions which have helped to bring this book to fruition.

First of all, we owe a prime debt to the Paul S. Cadbury Trust and to Eric Adams, its secretary, for the research grant which made it possible both to prepare this study and to publish this book.

We thank all the members and officers of the many local authorities throughout the country whose active interest and willingness to spare us their time gave us access to the information on which this account of their work is based.

The members of the Advisory Group are listed overleaf. Both corporately and individually, they have supported the inquiry splendidly by linking us with the three local authority associations, by offering advice, discussing the drafts, and also by actually drafting several of the chapters dealing with particular authorities. I wish to thank those members who wrote drafts for having put up so amicably with my editing; and Eric Adams and Stephen Humble in particular for so readily agreeing to withdraw their chapters, when it became evident that we had too much material for a book of this size.

Our thanks are also due to David Austin, whose cartoons have once again rendered the text totally redundant.

To ADVANCE, and its former director Tess Nind, we are greatly indebted for having placed at our disposal the organisation's resources, the most important of which was Rodney Hedley, who organised the survey, analysed the statistical results, administered the project, and contributed a chapter with unfailing good humour and efficiency.

Finally, I wish to thank Jonathan Croall and Jacqueline Sallon of Bedford Square Press for their efficient and easy collaboration; Denise John in Swansea and Sandy Derbyshire in London, who bore the brunt of the typing; and Glynis Atherton who helped the work so capably in so many un-assuming ways.

Maurice Broady

September 1988

The National Coalition for Neighbourhoods

The National Coalition for Neighbourhoods grew out of the report *Tomorrow's Community* which the National Federation of Community Associations published in 1979. It recommended that the Federation should seek to develop closer relations with other national bodies concerned with neighbourhood organisation and the Coalition was inaugurated in 1981 when the Association for Neighbourhood Councils joined with the Federation to promote the interests which they had in common. Soon, five national organisations had affiliated to the Coalition, which now, as a registered charity, has 14 national and regional bodies in membership. The term 'coalition' was deliberately chosen in order to indicate that each member organisation retained its autonomy and joined the Coalition to promote only those common concerns with which it could agree.

The Coalition aims to advance the following propositions:
- that the neighbourhoods in which people live are often the focus of strong feelings of personal identity;
- that they may also be the focus of social action, based upon that sense of identity;
- that neighbourhood action, in particular activity to secure better conditions, resources and influence among decision-makers, including self-help activity, is essential in a healthy democratic society; and
- that the importance of the neighbourhood is often ignored and needs to be better understood as an important element in social policy-making.

Further information about the Coalition may be obtained from the National Federation of Community Organisations, 8/9 Upper Street, London N1 0PQ; telephone 01–226 0189.

Members of the Advisory Group

Eric Adams, Secretary, Paul S. Cadbury Trust
Michael Ashley, Under Secretary, Association of District Councils
Glynis Atherton, Development Officer, National Coalition for Neighbourhoods
Mike Beazley, Honorary Senior Research Fellow, Birmingham Polytechnic
Maurice Broady, Chairman, National Coalition for Neighbourhoods
David Cliffe, Research Associate, Leicester University
Rodney Hedley, Research and Information Officer, ADVANCE
Stephen Humble, Director, Age Endeavour
Dugald MacInnes, Principal Administrator, Association of County Councils
Tess Nind, Director, ADVANCE
Robert Perkins, Assistant Secretary, Association of Metropolitan Authorities

1 Introduction

It might well be thought rather perverse for a voluntary organisation like the National Coalition for Neighbourhoods to be putting out an account of how local authorities in England and Wales are promoting community development; and that it should be doing so at this particular time. For local government is facing a period of unprecedented change. Even in the short period since this inquiry was started in 1986, its powers have been still further curtailed and its financial responsibility has been brought still more tightly under central government's control. During the past year, the Local Government Act has introduced competitive tendering, the Local Government Finance Act has laid the ground for the community charge, while the Education Reform Act has provided for schools to be taken out of the control of the education authorities and has given the Secretary of State over 300 reserve powers to intervene in what has hitherto been the purview of local government. In such ways the independence of our local government system is being undermined as control by central government is steadily increasing.

This process of change, though it has also been effected by many means a good deal less public than the introduction of new legislation, has been carried out in the full glare of public attention. But behind this very obvious change, another, quieter revolution has also been going on in the way in which many local authorities are trying to relate their services to their constituents. In one form or another, 'community development' has been gaining a steadily growing place in the way they run their affairs. In those local authorities that have adopted this approach, the effect has been to shift the focus away from simply providing a public service towards providing it with much greater sensitivity to *how* that service relates to the citizen in particular and, more generally, to the voluntary sector – that complex pattern of voluntary organisations and community groups – which operates within a local authority's ambit.

Granted, the interest which local authorities have increasingly begun to show in 'the community' has, to some degree, been encouraged by the growing financial constraints under which they have been obliged to operate in recent years. If social services budgets are to be cut, what better way to compensate than by co-opting the voluntary sector to provide some ancillary services? In the field of leisure and recreation, what is more appropriate in these circumstances than to encourage more people to use these facilities so as to make them more cost-effective? Attempts to appropriate the voluntary sector to meet the requirements of government have recently taken place in many other fields. Voluntary organisations have been expected to take on the totally inappropriate task of distributing surplus European Commission food while charities, in the manner of the nineteenth century, have been called upon to offer the poor the relief which they are being denied under the new social security legislation. If the independence of our major institutions, such as local government, the universities and even the press, is being jeopardised, why should the voluntary sector be exempted? A cynical councillor might be excused for supposing that this growing interest in community development reflected little more than the local authorities' expedient response to the financial difficulties in which central government's policies are placing them.

But he or she would only be partly justified in taking such a cynical view. Community development has been around for some time. Long before the present phase, in which rate-capping and privatisation have become the dominant themes of local government reform, social commentators like Professors Titmuss, Townsend and Abel-Smith were beginning to demonstrate in the late 1950s that the Welfare State had not by any means solved the problem of poverty and that 'equality of opportunity' was not a genuine equality for the underprivileged members of our society. The concern which this critique generated for trying to bring services closer to those whose needs were greatest showed itself in the Home Office's Community Development Programme which ran from 1968 and till the early 1970s in a dozen deprived communities in all parts of the United Kingdom.

At about the same time, the Town and Country Planning Act of 1968 required local authorities to encourage the general public to participate in the planning process, while the Seebohm Report of the same year advocated adopting a community development approach in the social services.

Central and local government have also had a long-standing commitment to community development by encouraging and, in particular, funding voluntary organisations. The Rural Development Commission, since its inception in 1909, has supported rural community councils and, under a variety of statutory powers, other government departments have funded the National Council for Voluntary Organisations and many other bodies, for which purpose, as well as to act as a link between voluntary organisations and government departments, the Voluntary Services Unit was expressly set up within the Home Office in 1973. Local authorities have long used section 137 of the Local Government Act 1972 to provide funds for such purposes. How to encourage collaboration between local government and the voluntary sector was also the subject of the Wolfenden Report on *The Future of Voluntary Organisations* which was published in 1978, and of the report on local economic development which the NCVO and the three local authority associations published in 1984.

How this inquiry began

It is clear, therefore, that this interest in community development on the part of both central and local government long antedates the difficult position in which local government presently finds itself. Nevertheless, it is undoubtedly true that local authorities are showing a growing interest in this field, and it was indeed one instance of this which led to the publication of this account. In November 1985, the Arts and Recreation Committee of the Association of Metropolitan Authorities (AMA) took the initiative to discuss with a number of national voluntary organisations, including the National Coalition, how collaboration between district councils and the voluntary sector could best be encouraged in the field of leisure and recreation. This conference anticipated by four months the publication by the AMA of its policy statement *Leisure Policy Now*, a document which showed that the association recognised the significance of the residential neighbourhood in the provision of public services. As the report noted,

Even where there is a national policy [for leisure], it will only be at the local level that specific provision of services can be decided in the light of social and economic changes as they emerge in neighbourhoods. The local authority is able to draw upon the initiatives and the resources of the community to develop a leisure policy and to create partnerships with the commercial sector and local sector and local voluntary organisations.

From the Coalition's point of view, what was especially interesting was this emphasis upon the importance of the neighbourhood as a source of initiatives and as a resource and upon the local authorities' creating partnerships with 'local voluntary organisations'. It matched our conviction that neighbourhoods are important bases of social action which are essential in a healthy democratic society and whose role in social policy needs to be much better understood. The Coalition accordingly wished to encourage the very interesting dialogue which the AMA had initiated. It was also interested in examining how far the local authorities in this and other fields of public policy were actually trying to take the neighbourhood into account. Since no general analysis of this kind was readily available – apart from Peter Willmott's *Community in Social Policy* – it was clear that an inquiry along these lines would make a useful contribution to the literature on community development, while also contributing to the discussions which the AMA had started.

No sooner had the idea been formulated, than the pattern of collaboration which has made this inquiry possible was established. Professor Broady, as chairman of the Coalition, agreed to direct and edit the study; Eric Adams of the Paul S. Cadbury Trust offered to seek his trust's financial support; and Tess Nind, who was then director of ADVANCE (Advice and Development in Volunteering and Neighbourhood Care) put at our disposal the administrative support of her organisation and the assistance of Rodney Hedley, ADVANCE's research officer, who is the co-author of this study. Several members of the Coalition's committee in due course agreed to carry out particular sections of the inquiry while the three major local authority organisations offered us their very positive support in what has been a very active and helpful working party.

The inquiry was divided into two phases. In the first phase, a questionnaire was sent out to all local authorities in England and Wales through the appropriate local authority associations. Of the 445 authorities, replies were received from 247 (56 per cent).

Of these, 109 (24 per cent of the total) stated that they carried out community development work and included notes, and frequently very informative papers, giving examples of the kind of work they were doing. These documents and comments proved particularly interesting. They frequently drew our attention to the limitations of the concept of community development which we had adopted. More generally, they indicated the kind of issues and problems which presented themselves to local authorities doing community development work.

The second phase of the inquiry was a study in greater detail of several local authorities which had worked out broad policies of community development which could be regarded as examples of good practice in this field.

From these various sets of data this account has been built up. In the following chapter, the general statistical analysis will be presented, together with a re-consideration of the concept of community development which was provoked by the local authorities' reaction to our initial definition. This leads on to chapter 3 which analyses the various interpretations which those authorities have given to the idea of community development. Chapters 4 to 7 present the more detailed accounts of the work being done by five local authorities: Crewe and Nantwich, a district council at a fairly early, but very positive stage of development; Thamesdown Borough Council and Newcastle upon Tyne City Council, examples of another district council and a metropolitan district with very advanced schemes of community development; and, finally, Cambridge City Council and Cambridgeshire County Council to illustrate what is being done collaboratively by two equally exemplary authorities. The last chapter considers some of the problems which local authorities face in adopting a community development approach.

This study seeks, then, to contribute to the dialogue which has been going on between local authorities and the voluntary sector since the Wolfenden Report was published 10 years ago. In the last couple of years in particular, both the Community Projects Foundation and the National Federation of Community Organisations have been running seminars for local authority officers and members. The Coalition hopes that this account will show what local authorities are doing in this field and, especially in the last chapter, help, on the one hand, to make the local authorities' difficulties better understood among voluntary organisations and community groups and, on the other, to help local authorities to understand the grounds on which they ought to extend their activities in this field.

2 What Is Community Development?

In England and Wales there are, in all, 445 local authorities. Of those which replied to our request for information, 109 (about a quarter) stated that they were carrying out community development in one guise or another, though, of this number, 36 (33 per cent), almost all of them district councils, did not actually employ staff in this field. However, a number of authorities which are known to be doing community development did not reply, even after being urged to do so on the telephone, and others may well have decided that the rather narrow definition of the field which we originally adopted did not include the work that they were doing. If these are taken into account – though we have no way of estimating their numbers with any precision – it is possible that more than a quarter, and maybe as many as a third of all local authorities are working in this field. Even so, it is a minority of local authorities which are doing so. In this chapter, then, we will present an overview of these authorities based on the statistical evidence which we collected; after which we will consider what the term 'community development' means, given the fascinating divergence between our own concept and the much broader and, as we will now argue, more acceptable definition which was implicit in many of the local authorities' replies.

The statistical analysis
Recognising, then, the risks of generalising from this non-random sample of local authorities, it is at least of interest to note that the county councils had, at 51 per cent, the highest response-rate, followed by the metropolitan authorities at 38 per cent. This relatively high rate of response is consistent with the fact that these authorities have responsibility for social services and education, both of which tend to have a community de-

velopment brief. It is also consistent with the findings of the National Institute of Social Work's survey in 1984 which showed that almost 50 per cent of the community work staff employed by local authorities worked in education and 30 per cent in social services departments; and of the Community Projects Foundation survey the following year which indicated that metropolitan authorities were taking the lead in supporting community work projects. As for the London boroughs, their response-rate of only 21 per cent would seem to be a serious under-representation of their interest in this field. However, the 20 per cent response from district councils seems validly to represent their level of interest, given that as many as 57 per cent of those which replied stated that they did not work in this field.

In 38 per cent of the authorities which replied, community development was regarded as of sufficient importance for a lead committee to oversee this work. In a few cases community development was a standing item on a main committee's agenda, but mostly the relevant committee was a specialist sub-committee of the council. Of the 41 committees, 34 supervised specialist staff and 28 had produced policy statements, mostly since 1982. The average size of their staffs was 12, with a typical ratio of managerial, administrative and fieldwork staffs being 2:2:8; the largest teams were found in county councils and London boroughs.

Whereas in county councils and metropolitan districts community development was mostly (60 per cent) located in social services and education departments, in district councils the favoured location was in housing or planning (25 per cent) and in leisure and recreation (65 per cent), a point of some interest given that commentators on community development tend to ignore this aspect of the work. In addition, the police were operating in this field in crime-prevention work with home-beat officers. Finally, six of the authorities located community development in the chief executive's department, where the average size of the staff, at 11.8, was next highest to education, where it was 16.8.

The political alignment of the local authority clearly affected the expenditure which district councils devoted to community development. The average number of staff employed in the 22 Labour authorities was seven, as against 1.8 in the 15 Conservative districts. (The remaining 29 districts did not employ staff in this field.) This is probably explained by the fact that these

Labour authorities covered mainly urban areas where the need for welfare provision was high. This is consistent with the fact that, according to CIPFA (Chartered Institute of Public Finance and Accountancy) statistics, Labour authorities in 1985/86 spent, at £74 per head of population, 42 per cent more on local services than Conservative-controlled authorities. In county councils, on the other hand, where there was an average of 18 staff per authority, no such relationship could be established; nor could any comparisons be made among metropolitan districts and London boroughs, since all bar one of them in our list were Labour-controlled. That community development tends to be used in work with deprived and underprivileged groups comes out clearly from our analysis. For though the one field that was most frequently cited, especially in the districts, was work with parish councils (21 per cent), almost all the other categories mentioned as being the specific concern of community development work were such groups, with work among ethnic groups, the elderly, children under five and disabled people predominating. It is interesting to note that, although district councils have no responsibility for education, five of them stated that they were embarking upon programmes for developing youth facilities. Surprisingly, community development work with unemployed people was mentioned by only 4 per cent of the authorities.

In encouraging local authorities to undertake community development work, the Manpower Services Commission's Community Programme appears to have had at best only a marginal influence. Thirty-seven out of the 109 authorities were involved in the Community Programme. District and county councils were much more likely to have adopted it than metropolitan and London boroughs, many of which, being controlled by Labour, were more likely to be opposed to the scheme. Most of the Community Programme projects, however, did not appear to be integrated with these councils' main pattern of community development and few, if any of these projects were directed by staff who were responsible for community development work. Thus, the Community Programme, though it was helping the unemployed on projects of 'community benefit', was not contributing materially to community development policy or practice.

Forty-four local authorities in our list funded workers in voluntary organisations and this was common to all kinds of authority. On average, they funded six workers who were typically deployed in three organisations. Voluntary organisations appear generally to be funded on an *ad hoc* basis with grants allocated according to the merits of specific requests rather than within a broader grant-aid policy designed to encourage particular kinds of activity within the community. However, some local authorities seem to be beginning to develop clearer criteria for allocating their grants. In addition, many county councils devolved some, if not all of their community development functions on to county-wide rural community councils. Some counties considered these bodies to be particularly well-equipped to represent specifically rural interests, and especially village networks, in relation to all forms of statutory provision in their areas. Paradoxically, the possibility that there could be conflicts of interest between the county council and local voluntary and community organisations appeared to be more readily accepted in these rural areas than in urban ones where community development tended to be better supported.

Thus, to conclude: although half the local authorities replied to our request for information, rather fewer than half of those which replied were actually involved in promoting community development and in allocating resources to it. But even though it may be practised by only a minority – perhaps as few as a quarter – of all authorities in England and Wales, and though the levels of provision may be slight, this function is clearly well-established in one form or another and only in a few cases was it regarded as merely a marginal activity.

Two views of 'community development'

Behind all these statistics, however, another, more conceptual question is lurking. For, as the replies came in, it became increasingly clear that many local authorities were adopting a far broader definition of community development than the one which we proposed in our questionnaire. Our definition stated that it had to do with 'the way in which your local authority *deliberately stimulates and encourages groups* of people to express their needs; supports them in their collective action; and helps them with their projects and schemes'. In this definition, the focus of attention is upon local groups and the emphasis is upon *their* needs, *their* collective action, *their* projects and schemes. The starting-point is in the local community and the role of the local authority is seen as being to offer these groups stimulation, encouragement, help and support.

Now it is clear, as our examples will show, that many local authorities do in fact carry out these functions towards community groups within their areas. But it is equally clear that they also undertake many other functions which *they* regard as community development; and in responding to our request for information they frequently made the point that our definition was far too restrictive. They often stated that they were in fact doing community development but that they preferred not to make this the responsibility of any specifically designated officer since, as they saw it, it was an aspect of every officer's work: they all had community development as part of their brief. Thus, Northamptonshire County Council stated that 'all local teams have an element of community development in their brief though it is not the sole or main responsibility of any individual member'. Or Hampshire, similarly: 'community development as a concept is built into planning policies, joint projects to implement new development, older urban area policies, adult education, youth and community provision, recreation, libraries and social services'.

This 'generic' view of community development has the obvious disadvantage that what is everyone's function may in

practice be nobody's function. It may well be a linguistic ploy enabling a local authority which does not wish to appear to be doing nothing to claim, in fact, to be doing something. Moreover, since the term 'community' is self-evidently desirable, whatever it may mean, and since it is also a rather fashionable word, there is always the danger that it may be tagged on as a prefix to virtually any other activity simply so that its practitioners can appear to be up-to-the-minute in their thinking and, by conforming to an easily adopted linguistic convention, strengthen their standing in making claims upon limited resources.

Such scepticism, however, is not necessarily always justified. For many authorities which considered our definition too constricting nevertheless used the term 'community development' to refer to any effort on their part to relate their services more responsively, and thus more effectively, to the community at large. In so far as it also involved trying to meet more directly what the members of local neighbourhoods regarded as their needs, it tied end-on to the concept which we ourselves had started with.

The reason for this difference between these two views of community development is that local government and community organisations approach it from two different starting-points. Local authorities understandably tend to begin with their prime obligation to provide a service for 'the community'; community organisations with their desire to see people encouraged to take on responsibility for social action in their own areas. At one extreme, local government perceives community development simply as a means of supplementing its own service by co-opting volunteers to support its own professional social workers, for example, by doing work of a non-professional kind with their clients. At the other extreme, community workers wish to encourage local groups to define and meet the needs of their own communities. Thus, in our original definition of community development as 'the way in which your local authority deliberately stimulates and encourages groups of people to express their needs; supports them in their collective action; and helps them with their projects and schemes', the personal pronoun 'them' is repeated and is crucial.

Those (ourselves included) who are primarily concerned with stimulating this kind of local action stand in danger of taking a somewhat partial view of what community development is about by ignoring what is the local authorities' prime concern: to bridge the gap between themselves and their services and the people for whom they are intended. In his account of one of the earliest community projects in Britain, the Bristol Social Project, Professor John Spencer pointed out 25 years ago how essential it was to relate community development work being done in neighbourhoods with the wider political context within which it was taking place. 'Action research in the neighbourhood,' he concluded, 'if it is to be of maximum value, must be related to the pattern of civic policy-making and administration in a thoroughly acceptable way.' The community development projects of the turn of the 1970s also recognised, though in a rather more aggressive idiom, that action within the local community could only be effective if it was complemented by parallel action in the wider political system. The point which came out of both of these projects perhaps needs to be reiterated: that community development involves both the local community and local government.

In our view, therefore, community development includes both local groups defining and meeting *their* needs as they perceive them and local authorities seeking to make their services more responsive to local needs. Local democracy entails both. That the emphasis of community workers should be upon giving power to local community groups may well be a necessary reaction to the tendency of local councils to regard their function as being to provide services *for* their residents. But residents organise themselves (in tenants' associations, for example) in order to affect how those services are provided and to have some say in how they are managed. So when a local authority itself seeks to make its services more sensitive to local needs and to encourage local people to participate in managing those services, this is no less an aspect of 'community development'. The broad definition of the field which Peterborough City Council, for example, has adopted expresses this wider conception very well indeed. 'Community development' it states,

is a service which seeks to act as a bridge between the local authority and local communities; it also strives to develop formal and informal contacts between departments and other agencies; and to assist local groups to define and meet their own objectives.

A continuum of community development

These conceptual issues, though they are different from practice, are not 'academic' in that pejorative sense of the term which means unrelated to practice. 'There is nothing more practical than good theory'; and these more theoretical questions arise with particular force when local authorities, which may have encouraged a wide range of community-related activities in various departments, come to consider, for example, whether they should be brought together into a special unit and, if so, where it should be located within the authority's administrative structure. So it is not surprising that a very helpful classification of community development should have been found in a report on community work which was prepared in Newcastle upon Tyne three years ago when this kind of question was being debated. In this broad definition of the term, community development is divided into six categories that range along a continuum which extends from the direct provision of community facilities all the way across to community self-government. The central criterion in this classification is the degree to which the residents of a neighbourhood influence and control the decisions that affect their locality.

Community provision is the first way in which local authorities deal with local needs. Chartered as they are to provide services and facilities for their citizens, their first response to the social deficiencies in housing areas was to provide certain social facilities. When new housing estates were built, they often lacked simple amenities such as shops and meeting halls, and tenants' associations sprang up to campaign for them to be provided. One common response was to provide community centres or tenants' rooms. Many local authorities which regarded providing facilities as their sole responsibility did little else, but others also provided wardens to run the centres. In making these wardens responsible to a committee of the council itself, however, and not to the committee of a self-governing community association, they failed to see that such centres, if managed by an association of local residents and users, could also serve an important role in social and political education. In many cases, the authority's responsibility for providing a facility prevented its seeing that it might also have a responsibility for encouraging citizenship as well.

The second stage might be described as community consultation. Here, members of the community are encouraged to attend public meetings or to join consultative bodies in order to express their opinions about what the public authorities plan to do in their areas. But while public opinion is actively sought by the local authorities, this tends to take place at the initiative not of the community itself but of the authority and to deal not with the community's own plans and proposals but with what the authority considers should be done in the locality. Thus, in this limited sense of the term 'participation', the crucial question of 'at whose initiative does the participation take place' is obscured as the community is invited to dance like a puppet on the local authority's strings.

Third comes *community co-option*, in which members of the community, usually in their voluntary organisations, are encouraged to carry out activities and to take some responsibility for such things as providing an ancillary social service within a neighbourhood. Typical of this style of activity is where neighbourhood care groups, for example, are set up or, if already in existence, are co-opted by a social services department to provide a visiting service for the aged which it would be too expensive for the department to provide from its own resources and which, in any case, might be done better by a voluntary group.

The crucial factor that distinguishes these three stages of community development from the three that follow is that the source of the initiative has thus far rested with the local authorities, not with the community itself. The second group of three points up the ways in which, in differing degrees, the initiative resides primarily within the local community which also begins to take on some active responsibility for managing its own affairs.

In *community management*, the members of a community assume responsibility for managing their own affairs, as in a community centre or a neighbourhood resource centre, but usually within a fairly specific and delimited framework laid down in accordance with the local authority's policy.

More active, and with a broader focus still is stage five, which might be described as *community action*. Community action is usually entered into in order to fight an issue, either by opposing a proposal put forward by the authorities or by urging them to do something to meet a local need, or else to advocate some change in the provision made at local level. Under this head come those attempts that are made to give disadvantaged groups a more effective say in local decision making. The tenants' association is perhaps the most obvious agent for this kind of action. This is the aspect of community development which is most likely to provoke adverse reactions from members and officers of local authorities since it involves people participating in local affairs not at their instance but as an expression of the views of the local people themselves.

Finally, there is *community control*, in which the local group has a responsibility for fund raising and an ability to take action in its own right as a fully autonomous body. Organisations such as parish, community and neighbourhood councils and some community co-operatives fall within this category.

A further point needs to be made about the scope of community development work. In considering why community development should be encouraged, a distinction must be drawn between justifications that are specific and those which are more general. What this means can be seen in the first two sentences of the *Working Statement on Community Development* which has recently been adopted by the Standing Conference on Community Development. The second sentence states the general justification: that 'Community development is about the active involvement of people in the issues which affect our lives. It is a process based on the sharing of skills, knowledge and experience.' This should be compared with the first sentence which defines community development as being uniquely concerned with the under-privileged. 'The constituency of community development', it states, 'is among the powerless and the disadvantaged'; which is amplified in the further proposition that 'the first priority of community development is the enabling of those who are traditionally deprived of power and of control over their common affairs'.

This particular interpretation of community development, important and valuable though it is, is nevertheless only one specific and partial justification of this field of activity. It is one which community workers are particularly prone to adopt since they are frequently motivated by a desire, through community work, to contend against social injustice – discrimination, oppression and inequality – and to redress the inequalities of power and access to resources which characterise society. It is also endorsed by many local authorities which, faced with increasingly severe financial constraints, wish to focus their resources on those who are in greatest need.

A theory of pluralistic democracy
This justification for community development, however, is only one among many such justifications. For the process of encouraging local groups to participate more effectively in order to

achieve their own purposes is a desirable goal, whether or not it leads to less discrimination or more equality. By the same token, it is desirable that local authorities' services should be better attuned to local needs, whether or not those needs are those of ethnic minorities in inner cities or of the relatively well-off in residential suburbs. Community development in our local authorities, therefore, needs to be placed within a broader framework than that proposed by the Standing Conference's declaration.

It is justified, in the first instance not by its role in achieving any specific set of political objectives, however laudable, but by its relevance for a more general concept of local democracy. The Association of Metropolitan Authorities' report on community development rightly considers that local government should complement its traditional function of providing services with that of 'enabling' other people and other organisations to contribute to local development. Decentralising services, promoting local forums, making social work and health care more locally available, encouraging play-groups and self-managed youth projects, making more effective use of schools for communal purposes: these are some of the activities which local authorities have promoted in this field, which we will consider in the following chapters. Local authorities are concerned with how they may deliver services more effectively by relating them more carefully to the needs of local neighbourhoods and by involving their citizens more closely in that provision. The *prime* justification for all this is not that it will help particular deprived groups in society, though local authorities may well be fully justified in such a concern, but that more responsive services are better services and that the more fully people participate in providing them, the better a democracy it will be.

Community development, accordingly, is based upon certain political principles. First, it is undertaken within a democracy. Democracy is a way of securing the broad consent of the people to the government which exists in order to serve their needs. These needs are met by services which cannot be provided by each individual separately but are better met corporately by a public agency. These services are likely to be more efficient when they are more responsive to people's actual needs; and community development is a method which enables the people to be more closely involved in their provision.

But providing services is not the only function of local government in a democratic society. In a pluralistic democracy, the government is recognised to be only one, if perhaps the most important, of the many organisations which should have the responsibility for taking initiatives that contribute to the public welfare. Voluntary organisations and community groups are also agencies through which people may provide for social needs to be met, within the framework set by the pattern of statutory provision. This kind of enterprise ought to be encouraged in a democracy, partly because better provision for meeting needs can sometimes be achieved in this way than by relying on the state's services and partly because people will learn more about democratic practice by taking responsibility directly in such organisations. Local government therefore has an important role in enabling these organisations to achieve their goals where these are clearly in the public interest. Community development is concerned to encourage people to share responsibility for social provision and with enabling them to participate in providing services for the community, either in association with statutory authorities or independently.

Finally, although the close-knit communities of earlier days have mostly been superseded, as increased mobility and rising standards of living have changed the restricted economic basis upon which they rested, the neighbourhood still remains a focus of social identity and a basis for common action which it is the purpose of community development to support and encourage. It is concerned with engaging people's skills, knowledge and experience so that they can take initiatives to influence and, at best, control the issues which affect them. Because a democracy should also be a just and fair society, community development is particularly concerned with seeking to help those groups which are less privileged or which suffer from discrimination.

This theoretical position, stemming as it does from a concept of pluralistic democracy, makes it possible to relate together in one perspective community development as bridging the gap between local government and the citizen and community development as encouraging local voluntary and community initiatives. To that extent it justifies the continuum of community development practice which precedes it in this account. Though admittedly rather bland and over-simple, this continuum nevertheless defines a wide, but progressive field of community development practice, ranging from community provision to community management, action and control. It allows us to accept as useful the provision of a community centre or village hall which, though a very limited form of community development, is nevertheless important and desirable, without in any way weakening our recognition that community development, at its best, has to do with encouraging autonomy in community organisations. For the provision of a community centre is only the first step along a continuum of activity that leads through to a still more desirable stage in which a local authority, having encouraged a community group or a voluntary organisation to find its feet and having put resources behind it, then encourages it to be run by its own independent committee, setting its own policy, within the essential constraints of public accountability. This catholic approach is also diplomatic in that it recognises that local authorities will move into this relatively new field gradually, and at their own pace. The idea of a step-by-step progression is far more likely to encourage them to adopt a community development practice and then to extend it than would a dogmatic concept that is too tightly defined.

3 Community Development: Varieties of Interpretation

With these conceptual issues defined, we can now turn to consider in greater detail what approaches are actually being adopted by local authorities under this heading. Though the six-fold classification affords a useful general framework for analysing what happens in practice, the interpretations of community development vary department by department. A local authority is not a monolith. Like most institutions, it consists of a relatively loosely connected structure of separate departments, each with its own distinctive function, pattern of organisation and way of operating and each subject to a differing range of external, professional and political influences. So interesting though it would have been to analyse community development activities strictly according to our theoretical continuum, this would in the event have been confusing and somewhat unrealistic.

An active concern for community development is found in only a minority – perhaps a third – of local authorities in England and Wales. But even among that minority, to judge from the questionnaires that were returned to us, only a third at the most are extensively involved in this field. The rest do community development work only in one department or simply place the responsibility for community development on to other authorities. Cornwall County Council, for instance, considers that it has acquitted itself of this aspect of its work by grant aiding the rural community council, while Bracknell, surprisingly for a district which incorporated a former New Town, regards community development as a function of Berkshire County Council.

Community development as liaison with parish councils

The term 'community' is certainly ambiguous. For whereas, in the Coalition's original usage, it refers expressly to non-statutory bodies, distinguishing in a pluralistic fashion the state and voluntary agencies, many local authorities, when they speak of community development, appear to mean assisting other bodies with statutory powers, such as parish councils. Tewkesbury claims to have 'a great amount of community contact'; but this only appears to involve consulting parish and town councils about planning applications and recreational facilities and providing footpaths under a Community Programme scheme. Neath similarly maintains links with its local, statutory community councils, as does Alnwick with the parish councils. Some districts have designated liaison officers to maintain these contacts or, as in Test Valley, to act as the secretary of the 57-strong Association of Parish Councils. But this district, like many others, is not disposed to go further and to offer equivalent support to the other non-statutory organisations within its area. 'The Council', states the chief executive, 'recognises the value of the work undertaken in the "voluntary sector" and is willing to encourage and support various organisations but not to the extent of providing a "Community Development Officer".' In a somewhat firmer statement of the same kind of approach, Slough states categorically that 'the Council doesn't fund projects run by non-statutory agencies'. Certainly, parish and town councils are much closer than districts to local communities, so that it is easy to understand why many district councils consider liaising with them to be 'community development'. But this is really a very restricted definition of the term since it takes no account of the wider structure of the community in which people organise community organisations and voluntary bodies, with which community development is primarily concerned.

Community development as providing facilities

One of the simplest interpretations of community development in this wider sense is for the local authority to provide amenities or facilities for people in residential neighbourhoods to use. The community centre, for example, was a way of meeting some of the social needs in municipal housing estates that had been built under the housing legislation between the wars; and it was incorporated as a social focus for the 10,000 inhabitants of the 'neighbourhood unit', which constituted a basic concept in planning new housing areas and new towns immediately after the war. In the fifties and still more in the sixties, when planners and architects, excited by the possibilities created by urban growth, were becoming increasingly committed to large-scale, high-density development, these ideas lost their force. In more recent years, however, when smaller developments more in tune with the human scale are once again appreciated, the provision of community centres has become an important element in some authorities' concept of community development.

Especially in the field of leisure and recreation, local authorities have been increasingly anxious to make their provision of facilities more cost-effective. Traditionally, they have seen it as their duty to provide buildings and other amenities for sport and recreation. But they have become aware of how restricted is the range of people who make use of these facilities. Stimulated also by the concern of bodies like the Sports Council, they have more and more sought to encourage people to engage in sporting and recreational activities who are not necessarily interested in conventional competitive games. All these factors have encouraged a concern to widen the use of leisure and recreational facilities.

Local authorities, accordingly, are anxious to relate the provision of those facilities more closely to local neighbourhoods; and this has led many authorities to rediscover the importance of community centres and village halls. Peterborough, for example, has long had a policy of providing community centres in residential areas, in which community workers would be based in order to provide 'professional support to volunteers who were trying to meet the needs of their neighbourhood'. As the number of community centres has increased while the complement of community workers has gone down, the importance of these centres in the social development of the city has grown. Blackburn first began to provide community centres, with the support of Community Programme workers, as recently as 1985. However, in a wider *Review of Community Services* in late 1987, it proposes to build a number of new community centres, as part of its new policy of supporting the voluntary sector, and recognises 'the need to support established and evolving Community Associations'. The report notes that 'the public's need for better provision has increased because of the greater amount of leisure time people have, either enforced or voluntary'. It acknowledges that

neighbourhood areas need a base available to anyone locally without restriction where individuals, groups and local organisations can meet, which can be a base for a wide range of activities and community events thus helping to generate community spirit, mutual assistance and bridge gaps between different generations, races, creeds and between those who have jobs and those who do not.

Similarly, East Staffordshire wishes to encourage 'a switch in emphasis to neighbourhood facilities', in the form of community centres or village halls for which there is a clear need in many wards and parishes.

These examples demonstrate that, while many authorities have long since recognised the importance of providing such social amenities, many more are coming to appreciate that they are essential for the social development of their communities. But if the provision of a community centre was once thought to be a sufficient response to local needs, nowadays attention focuses quite as much upon the questions of how local people can best be encouraged to manage those facilities for themselves and how they can be used for more outgoing work within the wider community.

Community development as decentralising services

This concern to relate leisure and recreation more closely to the local neighbourhoods is one aspect of a more general interest which a growing number of local authorities are envincing in decentralising their services. Though usually considered in relation to specific services, of which community education, social services and housing are as significant as recreation and leisure, there are a number of authorities which have decentralised, or are considering decentralising their services more generally.

At its simplest, decentralising services grows out of a desire to make provision more cost-effective and user-friendly. In the social services, the idea of the patch system of local working derives in part from the tension between ever-increasing case-loads and fixed or ever-diminishing resources. The policy, first advocated in the Seebohm Report in 1968 and then in the Barclay Report in 1982, of forming local partnerships with voluntary organisations and informal carers in the community is therefore regarded as valuable not only because it is thought likely to provide a better service for the client but also because it can in effect bring additional resources into social work practice. The growing demand for leisure and recreational facilities at a time when resources are declining has also provoked a good deal of rethinking about service delivery during the last 10 years which has led away from centralised provision towards seeking out local needs, involving neighbourhoods in defining those needs and encouraging volunteers to help in that provision. In the education service, community education has been intended to bring the adult educational and youth services into closer and more effective contact with the local communities they are there to serve. At its most basic, 'community education' simply means co-ordinating the provision of schools, the youth service and adult education so as to ensure, as a Northumberland County Council report puts it, 'that maximum use is obtained of school buildings and equipment by the public' and 'that the school is regarded as a major focal point for the whole community'. The recent report of a working party on adult education in Humberside also argues for integrating adult education into five further education colleges which would themselves operate through 17 smaller centres 'responsive to the needs of the communities in which they are placed'. These services have in the past mainly been attuned to the needs of people who were prepared to attend formal classes, usually in the evenings. Now it is recognised that the education service should become much more accessible to people, and especially to disadvantaged groups who have hitherto not made many claims upon it.

These efforts to decentralise particular services, however, are now being complemented by much more ambitious projects for decentralising the whole range of local authority services to local neighbourhood offices. The intention is to improve and extend the provision of these services, the better to serve local communities by making them more accessible and more related to their actual needs. It is the London Borough of Islington that has been in the forefront of this development.

When a new Labour council came into office in Islington in 1982, it immediately began to work out its manifesto commitment to decentralise its services and, by late 1986, it completed this programme with the opening of its twenty-fourth neighbourhood office. Before 1982, many departments had already begun to operate through local offices – 10 in the case of social services, six with estate management – but they all continued to be administered centrally. The new council, however, wished to implement a more thoroughgoing policy of decentralisation, partly for the general political reason that 'at a time of increasing centralisation and government cuts local democracy can only be strengthened by delivering good services and by drawing the public into decision making'. More pragmatically, decentralisation was intended to improve local services by making them more accessible to the people who used them and more account-able to local needs and priorities.

Islington is a relatively poor borough with dense housing, a high proportion of it in council estates, and a large ethnic population. It has been divided into 24 neighbourhoods, each with a population of about 6,500, which now have specially designed neighbourhood offices serving an area with a radius of 10 minutes walking-time. To man them, over 600 staff have been relocated, mainly from central offices, and 300 additional staff have been recruited. In particular, the hitherto rather haphazard deployment of the three or four community workers who were employed by the social work teams has been changed. There are now 24 such workers in the Chief Executive's Depart-ment, working in each of the neighbourhood offices, who are beginning to work out a more coherent community development practice as the borough is moving towards a community develop-ment policy for the area as a whole.

Each neighbourhood office comprises, first of all, four decen-tralised departmental teams from the Chief Executive's Depart-ment, which includes welfare rights and community workers, and the Housing, Social Services and Environmental Health Departments, each under a neighbourhood officer. There is also an area repair team from the Building Works Department. Since it would have been difficult to have nominated any particular officer to take charge of the work of all the departments operat-ing from each centre, there is no overall manager, but the four neighbourhood officers are expected to co-operate with each other in running the centres. However, the neighbourhood officer from the Chief Executive's Department is responsible for co-ordinating the work of each office, for managing the building, for making contact with the local community and servicing and supporting neighbourhood forums. The offices include accom-modation for their staff and for building-works employees and other neighbourhood-based workers like home-helps, care-takers, street-sweepers and gardeners. There are also waiting-areas for the public, children's areas, public telephones, inter-viewing rooms and facilities like typewriters, photocopiers and duplicators for local groups to use.

The effect of these changes has been to bring to each locality a more co-ordinated service. Thus, all the functions of the Housing Department, such as advice, lettings, transfers, rents and housing benefits, as well as estate-management which was always locally-based, are dealt with in the neighbourhood offices. Similarly in the Social Services, the neighbourhood officer is responsible both for field services and for all the day and residential establishments in his area, which used to be administered centrally; while direct labour, which was formerly organised from a central depot, is now devolved to 16 teams which are also based in the local offices.

There still remains, of course, a bureaucracy. The social services are organised in districts of four or five neighbourhoods under an assistant director and environmental health in six clusters of neighbourhoods under a principal officer, based in one of the neighbourhood offices. Specialised functions, such as race relations, trading standards and pest control, which are too small to decentralise, operate from a central office while support and advisory services, like lawyers, accountants, architects, engineers and valuers, have been grouped in a new department and divided into teams of professionals working in sub-areas consisting of several neighbourhoods. Finally, the Decentralisation Co-ordination Unit, based in the Chief Executive's Department, which contains specialists in personnel, finance and welfare rights and deals with research and information as well, manages the department's neighbourhood staff and co-ordinates policy and management issues among the central departments.

These developments are sometimes related to wider proposals which aim to give the local residents a much greater say in how these decentralised services are run. As will be seen, the democratisation of local government tends to be regarded as a corollary of decentralising services. This is similar to the way in which, in a much smaller field of activity, councils have moved well beyond simply providing social and recreational facilities and are nowadays no less concerned to find ways of helping the people who use them to manage them for themselves. Thus, the self-management of buildings, to which interpretation of community development we now turn, will be paralleled by the section later on which deals with 'community development as extending democracy'.

Community development as the self-management of buildings

The interpretations of community development which have so far been described have been concerned with the ways in which services and buildings should be organised in residential neighbourhoods. If that were all that was involved in community development, it would still be an expression of the traditional local government approach that its obligation is to make provision – in this case, of services or physical facilities – for people who are assumed to be passive recipients of that provision. But that would be a very restricted conception of what 'community development' involves; and in fact most of these projects also try to associate the users of such facilities more effectively with their operation, at the very least by seeking their advice on how the provision should be made, at best by encouraging them to participate much more actively in managing, and even controlling this kind of project.

Some of the earliest attempts to encourage self-management were to be found in community centres. Provided with grants under the Education Act 1944, they were recognised to have not only a social but an educational function by helping people to understand through practising it what democratic self-government meant. As a report from Scunthorpe clearly puts it, it was expected that, by running their own community associations,

quite ordinary people who most often feel far removed from the formidable machinery of state could learn more of the process of making rules and of the importance of heeding them whilst at the same time taking into account the views of other people and acting within the framework of a given constitution.

The simple provision of a building in which meetings and social activities could take place was therefore complemented, in the best practice, by allowing the building to be managed by association of those who actually used it. Hence the crucial distinction between a community centre and a community association.

This is, in effect, the paradigm of all those partnerships that in more recent years have grown up between local authorities and user-organisations, in which the local authority provides a building and possibly staff and other support, both financial and in kind, which are then managed by a local committee. Thus, Dacorum, in outlining its leisure services policy, states that it will provide 'either all or part of the cost of a community centre', if the need for it can be demonstrated and no suitable alternative premises are available. It will also offer grants or loans for associations 'to acquire, lease or develop' their own centres and 'consider making a grant towards the running costs of community building'; all in the expectation that the premises would be leased to trustees so that a community association would actually manage the centre, with the local authority retaining only the right to nominate representatives to its management committee.

Community development as consultation and participation in service delivery

Self-management is relatively easy to arrange in one building. Where wider areas of public policy and local government administration are concerned, however, community development tends to be interpreted in a rather more restricted fashion as consulting with local people and organisations about issues of common concern to the local authority, voluntary organisations or the ordinary residents of an area. Authorities such as Thamesdown and Harlow, for instance, have carried out surveys *ad hoc* to sound out local opinion on matters affecting public policy.

A similar *ad hoc* consultation in the Priority Estates Project in Leeds was carried out in a series of small, intimate meetings with the residents of a post-war estate to enable them to define and meet its needs and to improve the estate by allocating more resources to it and by co-ordinating its services. As a result of this consultation, various departments acted immediately to deal with the many complaints that had been made. A working party was also set up, comprising housing officers, local councillors and representatives of trade unions and the tenants, to consider how to improve the repair of council houses on the estate. There is also a network of Housing Liaison Consultative Committees, convened and serviced by the Housing Department, which are attended by councillors and tenants' representatives. Indeed, since the Housing Act 1980 required local authorities to consult with their tenants, housing departments have often taken the lead in supporting and consulting tenants' groups. As Barnsley's housing director states, it is becoming 'an increasingly important element within his Department's management of its estates, to actively encourage and work with Tenants' and Residents' Associations'.

Local consultative forums have been encouraged by many other local authorities, of which Northampton is a particularly interesting example. There, the borough council in 1985 took over from the former Development Corporation the town's possibly unique pattern of residents' councils. The 12 councils which were then in existence, and which are organised into a borough-wide federation, have a constitution similar to that of a community association. Although some residents wanted only one neighbourhood organisation both to represent them and to organise social activities, both the Development Corporation, and subsequently the borough council, encouraged the view that the residents' councils should function primarily as representative bodies, though some do in fact organise social functions as well. The possibility of constituting themselves as urban parish councils was considered but was turned down because they would then have had to pay for a clerk and because the residents considered their interests would be best represented by an organisation that was independent of the structure of local government. The Development Corporation, for its part, expected that, over perhaps 10 years or so, these councils might have taken on a managerial, as well as a purely consultative role, with responsibility for maintaining the property, and that they might even have developed into a tenants' co-operative, leasing the housing estates on a collective basis. There was little evidence, however, that the councils wanted this responsibility, so that the residents' councils remain 'in all but name the equivalent of Voluntary Neighbourhood Councils'.

The councils have been supported since their inception under the Northampton Development Corporation by a residents' liaison officer who has an advisory role and by modest grants to cover their basic running costs, though they are expected to become self-financing during the first 10 years. They have been keen to win 'an effective voice in the management of their houses and immediate environment', to encourage an active interest in local affairs and to bring local issues to the authorities' attention. These have mainly been matters affecting the housing estates, such as repairs, street lighting, sign posting, road safety and fire hazards but the councils' concerns have also extended to problems of unruly children, crime prevention and the design of housing. In addition, they have devised a 'tenants' charter' in association with the borough council, prepared papers for their members on the implications of recent planning and housing legislation and they have consulted with a wide range of statutory bodies, including the Anglian Water Authority, the police and education authorities and the community health council on which, through the federation, they are represented.

The local authority considers it preferable to deal with well organised bodies like this than with specially convened protest groups since, through long-term dealings with the authority, they are more likely to understand its problems and to be less abrasive. The councils, for their part, consider that they are better able to help their members by having a recognised status and regular relationships with the many departments of the local authority. In practice, they offer the authority a very good means of consulting and communicating with residents, which complements rather than conflicts with the work of councillors and other agencies.

The residents' councils are mostly composed of about 20 members from different parts of each estate, but the numbers involved have fluctuated and some councils have floundered and even folded, though they have in due course been re-established, as dealing solely with housing problems has proved insufficiently demanding. The borough council has therefore encouraged them to broaden their scope so as to discuss local services and community interests more generally, including 'environmental issues'. As the liaison officer has noted, while these councils depend 'ultimately on the commitment of . . . the local authority to resident participation itself ', it is the 'more broadly based Councils with a wider interest in their locality and with much more effective feed-back from the people they represent [that] are more likely to survive in the uncertain period ahead'.

In the field of community education, an extremely interesting development along similar lines to these is being worked out in Tameside, where community education forums are being set up in the hope that they will eventually be in a position to evaluate the provision that is made, identify needs and put forward proposals. This derives from the borough's concern to shift the focus of its educational service away from the formal courses which have been provided by the Adult Education Department of the College of Technology (which comprise 70 per cent of course provision), in order to meet the educational needs of the people in the very deprived areas of the borough who have not hitherto used the service to any large degree. It is therefore trying, as far as possible, to redeploy its adult education staff and resources from work in the college to work within the local communities: a redeployment which, it has been suggested, may be particularly congenial to a local authority which is already sharply divided by the very different ethos of the authorities from either side of the River Tame which were brought together to form Tameside in 1974.

Organisationally, the committees which dealt with adult education and youth and community work have been amalgamated into a Community Education Sub-Committee, responsible to the Educational Services Committee. These changes are intended to help local people become more fully involved in defining their own, formal and informal educational needs and to ensure that the local authority is able to meet those needs appropriately. The borough council proposes to focus its efforts in nine localities and, within those areas, on a number of priority groups which include adolescents, people who are unemployed or who wish to re-enter education as adults, especially women, members of ethnic communities, those lacking a basic education and 'those isolated from society through age or disability'. To this end, the education service is to be brought into closer contact with local groups and organisations since it was recognised that a positive relationship with the local community structure was 'necessary if those most in need of help through community education are to be reached'.

This means that a much closer and more active relationship with voluntary and community organisations is envisaged than in the simpler forms of consultation that have so far been referred to in this chapter. For the policy rests upon 'the promotion of common interest organisations and mutual support groups within the communities in order to provide a strong framework for the other aims' of what, significantly, is described as 'community education *and redevelopment*' [our italics]. Thus, the Community Education Sub-Committee will include members of the main Education Services Committee, of the staffs in adult education, youth work, community schools and community development, together with representatives of special interest groups and each community forum, and one from the Tameside Association of Voluntary Community Associations.

The most innovative aspect of these plans is the proposal to set up these community education forums. These will operate in nine localities, co-terminous with wards, each with a population of between 20,000 and 40,000. Their purpose will be 'to allow all those with an interest in community education provision to be involved in the debate on local priorities, and encourage a sense of "community ownership" of provision'. On each of these forums, as on the main sub-committee, there will sit, as well as the ward councillors and staff of local educational establishments, representatives of voluntary and community organisations, of users

and the management committees of maintained centres, partici-
pants in adult education courses and young people from the
neighbourhood.

These forums will be serviced by a staff team including a
community development worker and a youth worker, a community liaison tutor and an administrative officer, any one of whom
could take the lead role. The forums will control their own
budgets to which all the community education funds will be
allocated, and the staff teams, together with the chairperson of
each forum, will be responsible for putting together a community
education and development plan for the forums and senior staff
to consider. Schools, wherever possible, will be available for
community education and it is anticipated that a number of
community schools will be set up, each with a community
association or, at least, a user committee to manage it, with the
community associations being able, as of right, to use any resources that are not being used by the day-school.

Though the forums will have control of a budget, they will not
be part of 'the formal democratic structure of the authority',
which retains the 'ultimate authority' in making decisions.
Nevertheless, it is conceded that they will become 'weak, ill-
attended and unproductive' if they do not actually have 'substantial responsibilities and powers'. It is recognised frankly that
conflicts may arise between senior officers and a forum and its
local staff and it is proposed that they 'should be worked through
openly' and, if necessary, referred to the Community Education
Sub-Committee for a final decision.

In the cases which have been described in this section, the
local authorities themselves have recognised that, if their plans
for relating their services more closely to the neighbourhood are
to succeed, then they must develop a more positive relationship
with the community. To this end, they have set up new patterns
of administration to relate their services more effectively to local
interests and concerns: consultative committees, residents' councils and community education forums. Organisations such as the
Northampton councils, since they have been set up at the local
authority's instance, may be thought to be merely the puppets of
the borough council, especially when the council acknowledges
frankly that it prefers to deal with them rather than with 'specially
convened interest groups'. Their ability to represent the residents' interests, however, was as likely to be strengthened as to
be jeopardised by the fact that they were recognised by the

borough and enjoyed regular contacts with its officers. Indeed, the residents' liaison officer noted that the greater the range of their responsibilities the more likely they were to survive; a point very similar to the Tameside observation that, without 'substantial responsibilities and powers', the education forums would be ineffective. On the other hand, the residents' councils were unwilling to accept a managerial role or to develop into the tenants' co-operative which an over-enthusiastic Development Corporation had envisaged for them. In Tameside, it also seems that it will be much easier to devise a community education project than to find ways of getting officers to move out of the adult education centres into the neighbourhoods and of getting local people to join the forums. The authority is wise to recognise that, if the scheme works, it may provoke conflicts and it is prudent to make it clear that it retains the 'ultimate authority' in decision making.

Community development as co-opting voluntary organisations

If local authorities have sought to involve voluntary organisations and community groups in advising them on how the services which they offer might be more effectively related to local needs and local circumstances, they have also found voluntary organisations of use in supplementing their own services. This is found notably in the social services, in which it has been a long-standing practice to fund voluntary bodies to act as agents of the local authority in providing services, for the disabled or handicapped for example, for which it has a statutory responsibility. Large numbers of people have also been actively involved in voluntary social work. The Wolfenden Committee estimated that in 1975 about five million people carried out voluntary social work, making a contribution equivalent to that of 40,000 full-time workers. Given the steadily rising costs of providing services and the increasing case-loads which social workers have to carry, and at a time when central government has been placing increasingly severe constraints upon local authorities' expenditure, it is understandable that some social services departments should have sought more systematically to incorporate volunteers into their work. This has coincided with their increasing concern to enter into partnership arrangements with voluntary and community organisations in providing a more localised service in this field.

Hampshire County Council's Social Services Department illustrates very well the variety of practices adopted. Like many other authorities, it has for many years grant-aided voluntary organisations and it has also supported voluntary residential day-care establishments for adults and children, with a commitment of about £1.5 million in 1986 for services to specific individuals. In addition, it offers grants (£1.3 million in 1986) for services that complement those offered by the department, such as holidays and sports or outings for their client groups. Part agency-service and part complementary is the work of Age Concern, for example, to which the department grants £100,000 a year to provide 'services for the very vulnerable but also information, guidance, clubs etc. for many who would never come the way of the Social Services Department'. The decision to enter into a partnership with a voluntary organisation is made either because this is a better way to extend the service or because it offers better value for money. The department also enrols 'voluntary associates' who give their services free and are trained to assist professional social workers by visiting and helping the elderly, working in day centres and luncheon clubs and so on. Increasingly, the authority's policy has been not simply to respond to requests for support for particular voluntary initiatives, but to suggest developments which the voluntary sector might most usefully undertake.

An interesting coalescence of interests between the statutory and voluntary sectors has been the growth of 'community care groups' in Hampshire over the past 20 years. The first such groups were started in 1963 in Lee-on-Solent; they slowly extended in the sixties along the coast. Many were started by Anglican church groups in order to offer the simple but valuable caring that a good neighbour might do but they now have the support of people who do not necessarily belong to a church but who wish to help those in need in their communities.

These groups began *ad hoc*, raising their own funds locally, but they were in due course funded by the Social Services Department of the county council. After discussions with the three Anglican Diocesan Councils for Social Responsibility in 1976, however, the Department gave a grant for an advisor to be appointed to strengthen the work of the 20 groups which were then known to be in existence and to develop additional ones. Eventually a Co-ordinating Committee was also set up, comprising three representatives of the Diocesan Councils for Social

Responsibility in Winchester, Portsmouth and Guildford, who take the chair in turn, two from the Social Services Department and one from a health authority, together with all three community care advisors. Starting with one full-time advisor in 1976, since 1980, as the number of groups has increased, two part-time advisors funded by the county council and the health authorities have been employed by the Church of England, while Southampton is covered separately by an officer employed by the Council of Community Service, who is also funded by the county council.

There are now over 100 such groups throughout Hampshire, each varying according to local demands and resources, the skills of their members and the amount of time they can devote to this kind of work. Though membership fluctuates, each group is organised by a core of committed members, one or more of whom acts as co-ordinator, receiving requests for help either directly from the person needing it or from a statutory or voluntary agency. The co-ordinator then asks a group member to offer assistance or, where appropriate, refers the request to some other agency to deal with. In this way, therefore, they are able to provide a 'good neighbour service', responding immediately to local needs and emergencies and giving support to people at times of stress. They may run lunch and social clubs, community transport schemes and they may sometimes also set up community facilities to cater for special needs. They operate the more effectively as 'watchdogs over community welfare' to the degree that they are actively supported by the county's Social Services Department, as a complement to its social workers, and by the fact that the three advisors work under a joint county committee representing both the statutory and the voluntary bodies. The committee is responsible for allocating a modest grant – £8,000 in 1986/87 – to meet the groups' needs which helps the advisors to support existing groups, promote new ones, run training courses, publicise their work, liaise with other agencies and represent them in public.

Community development as local welfare planning

One typical method of relating social services departments and voluntary organisations is through agency agreements, under which the voluntary organisation contracts, against a payment from the local authority, to provide a specialist welfare function. The Hampshire example is interesting because the service is provided not by a semi-professional organisation but by groups within the community which are almost entirely staffed and run by voluntary workers. Though the county council can legitimately be said to have co-opted these groups to serve one of its functions, since the groups remain independent of the local authority, since the co-ordinating committee is equally balanced between the two sides and since the groups are willing collaborators in the work, this represents a genuine partnership between the statutory authority and the voluntary sector.

It is, however, of limited scope; and the role of the volunteers is very tightly defined so as not to infringe upon the functions of the statutory social workers. A much wider project in this same field is being undertaken by Arun District Council, which is promoting a pattern of community support for specific disadvantaged groups. This entails a much broader relationship and a closer partnership between the statutory authority and voluntary organisations. The district council is also making a substantial innovation by entering the field of social welfare that is the statutory responsibility of the county council. This parallels to some degree what was being done in Swindon from the 1950s onwards, where the town clerk encouraged the voluntary sector to provide a modest social service which he considered an expanding town needed but which, as a municipal borough, it was unable to provide statutorily.

Arun extends for 15 miles along the south coast, from Bognor Regis to its eastern boundary with Worthing. To the north, a rural hinterland gives onto the South Downs, while the coastal strip is predominantly urban, residential and heavily populated. An area much sought after by people retiring, 32 per cent of its population in 1981 (as against a national figure of 17.7 per cent) were old-age pensioners, while in many parts of the district the figure was higher than 40 per cent. Their numbers have been rising steadily in the last six years, especially of people aged 75 and over who have increased by 19 per cent in that period and who now constitute 13.3 per cent of the total population. The problems of this age group are therefore becoming increasingly significant. It has been primarily in response to the needs of this elderly section of its population that Arun's community support policy has been developed.

This policy reflects an unusually broad approach to the role of a local authority. The new Chief Executive, who moved into this office from that of borough treasurer with a brief to inititate policies to deal with unemployment and to support the elderly, made it clear in a paper on community support in 1984 that this 'would imply a change in the general philosophy of this Council'. The council, as he saw it, should not be concerned simply with what it was empowered to do but with what needed to be done in order to promote the well-being of its people and how then to do it. The environment in which it operated was changing.

If it wishes to be responsive to that environment it will see its role, not narrowly in the provision of limited and self-contained services, but more widely in demonstrating concern for and involvement in the overall pattern of life of the community and its general economic, social and physical well-being.

While in no way undervaluing the local authority's role as 'the main public instrument of local urban management', this forward-looking approach recognised that that role required it not to dominate, as the sole provider of services, but to take the lead in developing collaboratively, and especially in partnership with the voluntary sector, an integrated system for meeting local social needs.

The 'disadvantaged' in Arun, for whom the council planned to make particular provision by developing community support were the frail elderly, the long-term unemployed, the severely-handicapped and single-parent families. The elderly generally faced difficulties which were made more acute by their increasing frailty or severe handicap. In 40 per cent of those households which had pensioners living in them in 1981, the old people lived alone, most of them either widowed or divorced. Seventy-eight per cent of them lived in owner-occupied housing in which, unlike council or housing association premises, no element of care or support was included. As relatively few had cars, they were dependent for mobility on public transport or friends. In particular, the frail elderly suffered from difficulties in getting about, from social isolation and it was less easy for them to continue to run their own homes. It was quite clear that elderly people wished for as long as possible to remain in their own homes – 'their last expression of independence and dignity'. The council's concern therefore was to devise ways of helping them to do so.

'Community support' accordingly is 'concerned with assisting people to live their own lives more fully.' This means complementing the functions of the county council's social services department. Granted, a district council has no powers in regard to 'social services' thus defined. But it does have other powers which can be used to help the disadvantaged, notably in the fields of municipal housing, leisure and subsidising public transport; and it is also able to work with and to underwrite voluntary provision for social support. The meals-on-wheels service and lunch clubs, for example, are funded jointly by the county and district but are run by the Women's Royal Voluntary Service (WRVS). Similarly, the council offers grant aid for voluntary organisations to provide, among other things, play-groups, advice and information. However, there remained 'a gap between the care services of the social services authority and the largely unco-ordinated voluntary work undertaken in the community'. It was this gap that Arun sought to fill.

The district council aims then to strengthen its welfare support for the disadvantaged. The possibility of employing a special community development officer to relate to the voluntary sector was mooted, but, in the event, this was left as one function of an officer who was responsible for the community support programme as a whole. This programme rests upon developing in a co-ordinated fashion what both the local authority and the voluntary sector are doing. 'It is vital,' stated the research report on *Community Support*, 'that the links between the Council and the voluntary sector are maintained and voluntary agencies encouraged to develop in areas which are complementary to or in support of the Council's policies and programmes.'

The local authority's direct role is especially clear in regard to housing and transport. In accordance with the proposals made in that report, it has given priority to home improvement grants for the frail elderly and to providing alarm systems for them and for disabled people in both municipal and private housing. The system was set up by a working party representing the various statutory bodies, including the police, fire and ambulance services, the churches and other voluntary organisations which continue to be involved in its management, while some 1,500 alarms have been donated by private firms and voluntary organisations. Purpose-built day centres have been provided in Bognor Regis and Littlehampton while a mobile team has set up about twenty drop-in centres in schools, village halls and sheltered housing in other neighbourhoods and arranged for voluntary committees to run them.

This pattern of improved provision has been supplemented by

voluntary workers and voluntary organisations to which the council has extended grant aid support, which has risen steadily from about £15,000 in 1983/84 to £115,000 in 1988/89. The day centres, for example, are staffed by volunteers with one full-time worker in charge of each. The WRVS meals-on-wheels service has been continued and extended with the council's support and a pattern of street wardens or volunteer visitors set up under its aegis. Similar financial support has been provided for voluntary organisations to run community transport schemes in areas poorly served by public transport and for other organisations to provide a community information service.

The responsibility for developing and implementing these policies was originally placed with the chief environmental health officer. In the subsequent reorganisation of the district's administration, it is now divided between two officers, one a new appointment in the Housing and Community Care Department, who is responsible for work with disadvantaged groups, and the other in the Environment and Leisure Department, who deals with general community support.

Community development as general support for the voluntary sector

We have described the arrangements considered in a previous section as 'co-opting' voluntary organisations to help meet the complementary needs of a local authority's social services department. The term is not intended to be a pejorative since the groups that are involved are greatly helped by their association with the local authority and are willingly associated with it. This kind of partnership arrangement, so important an element in the pattern of a pluralistic democracy, has long been established in England and, to a lesser degree, in Wales, as a legitimate and desirable mode of organisation. It shows itself particularly in the financial support which local authorities give to the local development agencies in the voluntary sector in their areas, mainly the rural community councils and the councils for voluntary service.

Many authorities, however, have begun to develop more coherent structures for promoting the development of the voluntary sector. In some cases, such as Harlow, these have grown organically out of the social development departments of many of the original New Towns; elsewhere, as in Peterborough, Northampton and Warrington, the borough has taken over the responsibility for community development which had originally been promoted by the former Development Corporations. Other authorities have tried to bring some coherence into the various forms of community development work that have often been started *ad hoc* by several different departments, efforts which have led to a more general pattern of support for this kind of activity being considered, and sometimes implemented. Often, however, this development aims to encourage detailed field-work, especially among deprived or underprivileged community groups, and this will be described more fully later. Here, we are more concerned with the organisations which some authorities are developing to give broad support to community development work in their areas.

In Lincolnshire, for example, where the county council was already giving voluntary organisations about £200,000 a year in grant aid, the question of increasing its support for the voluntary sector arose from a review of its services for the elderly. This proposed that a voluntary services co-ordinator should be appointed to strengthen the links between statutory and voluntary effort in the personal social services. But this idea was superseded when central government announced that special grants were to be made available for setting up local development agencies, such as councils for voluntary service. The county council, supported by the volunteer bureaux in Lincoln and Grantham which wished to grow into councils for voluntary service with broader functions, applied for a grant for this purpose. In the event, the grant covered only Lincoln, where the functions of the volunteer bureau have now been incorporated into the newly established CVS. A new post in the Social Services Department has also been designated, partly to liaise with and deal with grants to the voluntary sector, in which the development of CVS in the five other social services districts is likely to be an important priority.

In this case, the initial move to support the voluntary sector grew out of the concern of the Social Services Department to find more volunteers to help the statutory services for the elderly. In Hereford and Worcester, on the other hand, the county council's policy has from the outset been to foster community development *per se* rather than community development tied to the functions of any one department. Thus, although it was the Social Services Department which nurtured an interest in this field, with the active support of its director, the position paper which in September 1981 proposed the establishment of a 'community development group' expressly stated that community development should 'not be over-identified or submerged in the existing identity of any specific department', since it was not about how any particular service was to be delivered. The fact that it had been closely associated with a sympathetic social services department had 'resulted in a preconceived and incorrect idea of the kinds of issues [it] was concerned with'; and it had 'led staff in other departments [into] feeling that it was nothing to do with them and [that it] had no right to be involved in their specialist areas of concern'. As a result, other departments of the county council seldom drew on the help which the council's own community development project had to offer.

Hereford and Worcester regard community development as a distinctive field of activity in its own right. Its work in this field had begun in 1975 in the rural part of the old Herefordshire, evidently as some kind of consolation to that county's wounded pride when it had been unwillingly amalgamated with Worcestershire in the reorganisation of local government the previous year. In its view, community development was concerned with involving ordinary people 'with all the insights, skills and time they can bring' in solving community problems. It fostered self-help by encouraging people to think creatively about local issues rather than reacting, usually negatively, to proposals emanating from outside their community. It sought to develop this potential within rural communities and to avoid crises developing by anticipating problems and encouraging people to meet them by a co-ordinated, and thus a more economical approach. This method meant focusing not upon single issues that were the responsibility of specific departments but upon an integrated approach to local problems. Since this means working across the boundaries of a variety of organisations and local authority departments, it was understandable that community development, as a function of the county council, should eventually have been placed in a separate section within the central administration.

When a separate Community Development Unit was set up in 1983, it was made responsible to the chief executive for carrying out its functions with and through the council's service departments. This was a time when the council was operating under severe financial constraints; and its establishment was greatly helped by the evidence that, when the resources of the county council were linked with those of voluntary organisations, other public bodies and charitable foundations, they were more than matched by their contributions. The unit consists of a community officer, a worker and an administrator. Taken together with the county council's grant-aid programme which supports the rural community council, and seven CVS and over 20 resource centres in towns throughout the county, this constitutes an innovative pattern of support for community development.

The unit's purpose is simply to help local communities to help themselves. Earlier work had shown that self-help is encouraged when people have access to well-informed local leaders, to resource centres and funds for supporting new initiatives and to a community development agency that can respond, quickly and flexibly, and with a worker who can help to organise activity, to support local groups dealing with social and economic needs and problems. The unit may offer either direct or indirect assistance.

Direct assistance includes marketing, financing and resourcing. The unit helps communities to find contacts, match local needs with available resources and to locate financial and other resources: marketing. It offers grant aid under small grants and capital grant schemes as well as through a community development project fund. It provides a training programme for CVS together with additional support, advice, information and a development programme: financing. Third, under resourcing, it makes available duplicators, typewriters and information through a network of local resource centres; it also supports innovatory projects that are delivered through the rural community council and offers training in management and marketing techniques in order to strengthen their activities.

Indirect assistance covers development, integration and innovating. By development, the unit helps the county council's service departments to assess and respond positively to community problems and enables those departments and community organisations to collaborate more closely. It has also recently helped to set up a forum of local development agencies. Integration involves linking local initiatives with national programmes and sources of funding; using the Community Development Fund to show that the county council supports such initiatives; encouraging information and advice centres, resource centres and local development agencies to collaborate more effectively by using information technology more fully, supported by the grant-aid scheme; training people in voluntary organisations in management and evaluation skills; matching local community needs with business resources through partnership schemes; and monitoring and co-ordinating the council's grant-aid programme. And finally, innovating means helping voluntary bodies to use local resources more efficiently and to become more responsive to pressing social issues and community needs by strengthening and extending the network of local development and resource agencies and by encouraging community leaders, business advisors, local government officers and volunteer organisers to act as well informed 'community development agents'.

Both county councils, in Lincolnshire and in Hereford and Worcester, are concerned to give the voluntary sector general support for their work. In both cases, they do so by encouraging local development agencies – CVS, rural community councils, volunteer bureaux and resource centres – to be set up and then by partly funding them. But Hereford and Worcester has taken a further and innovative step forward in establishing within the county administration itself a Community Development Unit to add further support to what these voluntary organisations are doing.

But there is another important difference to note. In Lincolnshire, the impetus to encourage the voluntary sector grew out of the social services department's review of services for the elderly, and it was intended to add the voluntary sector's contribution to the county council's work in that field. In Hereford and Worcester, on the other hand, though a similar emphasis also informs the unit's work, community development is no less concerned with encouraging local communities to take their own initiatives to define and solve their own problems and to meet their own needs.

The view of community development which the AMA's guidelines endorse is one which makes a very sharp distinction between community development and community service. For reasons which have been given earlier, we define community development rather more broadly so that it would certainly encompass services given to the community by voluntary organisations in support of the statutory services. Nevertheless, we consider the kind of community development which Hereford and Worcester has promoted to be especially valuable. This is because it goes well beyond giving voluntary organisations the opportunity to contribute to the statutory social services; it entails doing what the AMA considers specifically to be community development, namely involving the people themselves in defining their own needs and developing responses to their own local problems. In this case, the primary initiative lies with the local community or neighbourhood rather than with the statutory authority. To that extent, it is an aspect of democratic practice, to which interpretation of the field we may now turn.

Community development as extending democracy

In an earlier section of this chapter, we noted that some authorities had promoted major schemes for decentralising their services, of which Islington was the best example. In several of these cases, this pattern of decentralisation has been associated with the promotion of neighbourhood forums which have been expressly intended to extend the democratic control of local services to the people who actually use them. In this sense, community development has been interpreted as a way of extending democracy.

This concern grows, in part, from a belief that local services will be much improved if they are informed by local views and priorities. But some Labour-controlled councils also wish to reassert the importance of local government in the face of central government's efforts to reduce the power of local authorities by cutting their resources and restricting their powers. As a report of Harlow's Decentralisation and Democratisation Working Party puts it, 'if local government, and local communities, are to survive, their councils such as Harlow must win the active support of local people in defence of local services and jobs'. This is to be done by decentralising services and by promoting local democracy at the same time. Indeed, Harlow considers that there is 'an essential link' between the two and that the prime reason for decentralising services is to make it possible to extend democratic control. Since people generally are disenchanted with local government, feel distanced from it and 'do not feel they have any control over how it affects their lives', the council proposes to encourage their active participation in its operation by promoting these two inter-related policies.

The two authorities in our sample which have gone furthest in this direction are Islington and Harlow. However, neither of them has so far actually devolved power to neighbourhood organisations and both recognise that it will not be easy to do so. The Harlow paper notes that 'because of their present experience of the council and how it relates to them, it is unlikely that people will come forward spontaneously to take part in the new structures immediately they are set up'; and that a 'considerable amount of community development work' will be needed to encourage them to do so. Islington also recognises that it will take a lot of effort 'to draw in people who have not been used to expressing their views in this way'. It therefore expects to have to proceed slowly so as to learn from experience.

The logical connection which many advocate between democratisation and decentralisation is related to the frequently expressed concern that, if local councils or forums are set up, then they should be more than mere talking-shops but should have some real power to decide things. As the Islington report states, 'The public needed convincing that they would have real influence and that their views would be taken seriously'. For this reason, the report also commented 'that devolving decisions to local offices was essential to give people faith in [neighbourhood] forums'.

The Islington proposal envisages the local neighbourhoods themselves determining their own constitutions – questions like whether their membership should be by election, nomination or a combination of the two, for example – subject only to their being ratified by the council, which will 'lay down minimum conditions to ensure that forums are democratic, properly representative and accountable to local people'. Their primary role will be to express local opinions more effectively so that services and the allocation of resources can be improved by being more sensitively related to local needs. They would be empowered 'to spend money on improving their environment, on security for housing estates, parks and playgrounds and *will have a say in* [our italics] larger capital spending programmes locally'. For the rest, their powers will be limited to being 'consulted' about planning applications and requests for licences and permits and to being 'able to influence the way services are provided from their neighbourhood office'. Indeed, the Islington report expressly states that 'staff will be expected to act on their recommendations unless they are against council policy or illegal'. So far, about half of the 24 neighbourhood councils have been constituted. The next phase will be to devolve to the local management teams control of financial items like the £7 million repairs budget, the £2 million environmental programme and the social services team's projects, items which may only be spent with the agreement of the neighbourhood councils.

In Harlow, the proposals are rather more tightly defined. They envisage 16 neighbourhood committees based on existing ward boundaries, each of which would be serviced by a community development worker and have resources to cover publicity and administrative support. They would be related to eight neighbourhood offices dealing with housing, the environment, community development and welfare rights, information, recreation, cash payments and the servicing of neighbourhood committees. Each office would also act as a drop-in centre for volunteers and community groups and as a community resource centre.

'If neighbourhood committees were to be successful,' the working party's report states, 'then they needed to have real power and should not simply be consultative bodies.' They should comprise the local councillors, representatives of local community groups and directly elected local representatives, together with trade union representatives from the council's work-force. The report on decentralisation proposes that, over a period of time, the powers of the existing service committees should be gradually transferred to the neighbourhood committees while, at the centre, the committee structure should be redefined so as to retain only a resources and policy committee with such sub-committees as might be needed. Thus, while the neighbour-hood committees would have considerable autonomy so that the council would normally accept their decisions, the council as a whole would remain responsible for 'general decisions about policy and the allocation of resources and other areas of decision-making which it wished to reserve for itself '.

So far, although services have been decentralised in a number of local authorities, the policy of democratisation in this wider sense is still being worked out. It will therefore be several years before a definitive assessment of these proposals can be made. All that can be said at present is that every local authority that wishes to move in this direction, like Tameside whose commun-ity education forums envisage a similar though smaller develop-ment, appreciates that it will not be easy to get people to understand, and then to work on these newly formed neighbour-hood committees. They also recognise prudently that the local authority will be obliged to reserve certain powers and decisions to itself. Success in this field is not likely to be achieved without some conflict of interests between the councils and these local

committees. This, then, is at the more demanding end of the community development continuum. For that reason, and also because policies of this kind combine the provision of local services with an extremely interesting and important experiment in community education, it merits our particular support.

Community development as direct support of neighbourhood groups

Now promoting a decentralised pattern of local democracy, like many of the activities that have so far been described as 'community development', has to do with building new kinds of organisation. An organisation is a body with a clearly-defined constitution and structure that is set up to achieve specific purposes. It is understandable that statutory authorities, which are organisations in precisely that sense, should regard community development as being concerned with what might be described as linking organisations that seek to bridge the gap between themselves – the local authorities – and the communities which it is their business to serve.

These communities or neighbourhoods, however, are made up of groups; and though groups may also seek to achieve particular purposes and have constitutions, they are generally much less formally structured than organisations and in much closer contact with the people in the neighbourhoods in which they operate. Setting up linking organisations is dealing indirectly with these local groups. But community development also deals with them directly; and it is in this sense that the Coalition defined community development at the start of this inquiry. By 'community development' it referred to how a local authority 'deliberately stimulates and encourages groups of people to express their needs; supports them in their collective action; and helps them with their projects and schemes'. It is to this interpretation that we must now turn, with examples from Cleveland and Nottinghamshire County Councils.

This kind of community development work is mostly carried out in relatively deprived or underprivileged communities. It tends to be associated with positive discriminatory policies which aim to redistribute public resources in favour of those communities in which social need is most acute but which lose out still more because the local residents lack confidence in their ability either to articulate their needs or to take initiatives to try to deal with them. Community development work in this sense is therefore intended to help these people in particular to organise themselves in order to do this. Community workers, too, generally consider that it is in such communities that their work should be done, as an expression of their concern for social justice and redistributing resources. This is why the Standing Conference on Community Development expressly states that 'the constituency of community development is among the powerless and disadvantaged'. This approach is consistent with the concern of many local authorities, in a context in which financial resources are becoming increasingly tight and the disparities between rich and poor more acute, to focus those resources more effectively on those groups which stand in greatest need.

The work in Cleveland was promoted by Middlesborough but organised by the county council. It involved *one* neighbourhood worker working for the three years 1983–86 in a large inter-war council estate of some 1,800 dwellings where, in 1981, 40–50 per cent of the men were unemployed. Part of the estate had been cleared, part renovated and in 1983 a 10-year programme of selective demolition and rebuilding had begun. The purpose of the project was to encourage people to participate in this process of modernisation and redevelopment.

Neighbourhood work was defined as 'a short-term measure for improving communication and creating more cohesion in communities experiencing difficulties through change or deprivation'. It involved working with residents so as to identify their needs and get resources to meet them, and collaborating with the local authority and other agencies in order to make their services more sensitive to the community's social and welfare needs. The worker's role was that of a catalyst, supporting groups within the neighbourhood and introducing new ideas and projects while encouraging others to assume leadership roles within the community. The test of the project's success would be 'whether the improvements and developments set in train by the worker thrive and endure without his/her intervention and, indeed, after he/she has withdrawn from the area'.

What was achieved by one sole worker was necessarily limited in scope but none the less valuable. It is work that is slow and sometimes disappointing but which nevertheless makes a direct and tangible contribution to social well-being. Granted, the field which the worker was specifically appointed to till – acting as an 'honest broker' between the tenants and the borough council –

was the one in which least was actually achieved. Discussions between the council and one of the tenants' associations had already begun when she arrived in the estate. Nevertheless, as a co-opted member of the project officers' team, she was able to ensure that the associations were properly consulted. She also helped the tenants' associations to organise open meetings, prepare themselves more carefully than they otherwise might have done for discussions with the council's officers and to produce a leaflet about the financial aspects of the modernisation programme.

So much time would have been needed for one person to set up a much needed project for unemployed young people that it had to be ruled out as impracticable. For during the first year a good deal of time and effort was necessarily taken up with making contacts in the area and finding a base, Neighbourhood House, from which to operate. The worker was involved in strengthening the tenants' associations by helping them to produce a constitution, to amalgamate, and to avoid simply complaining but to begin to represent their members more effectively in their dealings with council officers. The associations were also encouraged to promote social activities and they agreed to man Neighbourhood House for a few sessions each week and took part in a tidy-up campaign.

The worker also got the council to agree to set up more nursery provision for under-fives than was originally planned. She supported an initiative to set up a junior football club by getting an equipment grant and persuading a local school to allow it to use its playing-field. She secured grant aid for a play-group for 9–13 year olds and set up a support group for volunteer play-workers. She was active in organising a welfare-rights group for which she arranged grant aid and training and recruited volunteers. Finally, she organised a luncheon club in the estate which brought together officers from various departments and services and representatives of voluntary organisations, churches and residents' associations.

Though some of these efforts were not as successful as might have been hoped, several of them were being capably run by local people by the end of the project. More generally, a useful, small-scale pattern of community organisation had been set up, with Neighbourhood House established as a thriving centre for all kinds of activities ranging from a tool library run by the tenants' association to the Social Services community care support scheme.

A wider community development project, which has also been carried out by a social services department, has been promoted by Nottinghamshire County Council. It is founded upon the conviction that this kind of activity is particularly relevant in the most deprived communities, where local neighbourhood groups should be encouraged to have a say directly in decisions that affect their lives, to define their own needs and to tackle their own problems by collaborating with other organisations. In this way, their potential for social action can be helped to find an appropriate expression and their self-confidence strengthened. 'Change for the better should be sought by means of co-operation, self-help, local involvement and improvement arising out of objectives agreed with community groups.' Action of this kind can influence the distribution of resources in favour of socially-deprived communities.

This sort of work, however, requires local groups to be well-organised and supported with direct help, advice and encouragement. This in turn calls for 'a confident, co-operative approach by the Department and its staff'. The community workers accordingly are expected to operate within a clear framework of policy and to plan their work carefully so as to help the groups concerned to achieve positive and practical improvements in their environment.

Though it is the Social Services Department which has encouraged community development since the early 1980s, this is quite different from 'social service' in the traditional sense of social workers dealing with individuals' problems. In the middle of 1986 therefore it became the responsibility of the Department's Community Division, one of four operational divisions, of which the other three deal with the elderly, the disabled and with children. The community support team consists of 19 community development workers operating in seven separate projects. There is also a quarterly meeting of the representatives of the community groups themselves.

While the community workers involved are 'expected to exercise their judgement and skills within the framework set by the Social Services Committee, the Department' and other committees on which they are represented, each project is managed by a local committee representing the local authority, the community workers and the groups with which they are working. In Bassetlaw, where the work 'is heavily loaded towards the wishes of the communities and community groups with which it [the team] works', the voluntary groups are expressly given a majority on the committee. In Nottingham City, on the other hand, where six out of the 19 workers are employed in the largest single project, a rather more formal committee meets monthly under the chairman of social services, with another county councillor, a city councillor and a representative of the groups with which the team works.

As in many other authorities that regard community development as a way of helping disadvantaged communities, it is accepted that the community workers will wish to help local groups to mount campaigns to persuade the civic and other authorities to change either their policies or their practice. Such 'campaigns' have won improvements in community health, sports facilities, and in amenities for the homeless and for battered women. But perhaps the major campaigns have been about municipal housing. Reductions in rents and rates have been successfully won and local councils have been obliged to make improvements by draft-proofing and energy conservation schemes, in one case with a capital expenditure of £3 million. Another campaign which was initiated by local residents' associations and which rallied the county council, the district councils, housing associations and MPs of both the major parties to its support, succeeded in preventing British Coal from selling miners' houses speculatively to the detriment of the tenants, many of them miners' widows, who were living in them.

But behind these more spectacular activities, work of a less obtrusive but no less important kind is also carried out. The community workers, for instance, have helped to ease relationships between local groups and the public authorities, which they have encouraged to set up housing liaison groups and similar bodies. They have helped residents to justify their representations to the local authorities by carrying out surveys into housing repairs that are needed and the needs that a day-care centre could meet. They have prepared reports on a mobile crèche, a booklet on women's health and a 'health and play pack'. They have helped local groups to set up community newspapers and advised them on how to organise resource centres and welfare-rights groups, and have run training classes in things like chairmanship and committee work so as to help local people to be able to participate more effectively in local affairs.

In these various ways, then, Nottinghamshire County Council, like Cleveland on a smaller scale, has seen community development as a way of fostering a closer and more responsive relationship between these deprived communities and the public authorities which serve them and of improving their circumstances by a modest redistribution of resources in their favour. Though this has given these areas additional facilities such as youth centres, resource centres and crèches, and has led to much-needed housing improvements being carried out, the significance of a community development method is that these improvements have been made in response to the definitions of need that have been formulated by the local people themselves. This procedure has encouraged them to make use of their own resources – of energy, work and intelligence – and to set up their own organisations to tackle the problems that they have defined. Thus, at the end of this process, there are networks of community organisations in the localities – tenants' associations, welfare rights groups, housing liaison groups, resource centres, most of them run by local volunteers – through which the residents are now able far more effectively to 'help themselves to help themselves'. In an even wider sense, through setting up these organisations and arguing for amenities, they have also in a very practical fashion learned a great deal about the practice of local democracy.

Conclusion

The foregoing examples have shown local authorities doing community development in a wide variety of ways. Their purposes are perhaps slightly less varied. Some local authorities have clearly entered this field in order to some degree to offset the restrictions that have been forced upon their services by central government's increasingly tight control of their finances. In these cases, their prime interest has been in maintaining a service. At the other extreme, especially where local authorities have sought to redress the balance of advantage in favour of deprived and underprivileged groups, the main focus of concern has been to enable those groups to claim greater power and more resources by more effectively participating in the political process.

There has been a tendency to polarise these two approaches. Certainly, local authorities have been prone to take the view that their role is simply to provide facilities and not to encourage civic participation; and there are undoubtedly many authorities in England and Wales which still subscribe to that view. We should not denigrate this approach. But in an era in which unemployment is high, leisure time increasing and both the number and proportion of pensioners is rising, boroughs like Blackburn are starting to appreciate the importance of providing community centres for their people. And in doing so, they are recognising the equal importance of ensuring that those centres are run not by the local authority but by independent community associations representing the people who actually use them.

An emphasis on service provision, however, can lead local authorities to take a fairly restricted view of the voluntary sector. Some social services departments, of which those in Hampshire and Lincolnshire are good examples, are apt to see voluntary organisations as valuable mainly to the degree that they can complement their own work by offering ancillary services of a non-professional kind. Nevertheless, though co-opted to the county council's service, the Hampshire community care groups were thereby enabled to do more effectively what they set themselves up to do. The organising of a CVS in Lincoln, though it presumably must meet the county council's concern to provide for the elderly, has nevertheless established an independent voluntary organisation in the town, from which the voluntary sector as a whole stands to benefit.

Similar inferences can be drawn from other services that have been cited. Housing departments have been encouraged to set up tenants' organisations which have given them a better method of consulting the opinions of their tenants in housing matters. Leisure and recreation departments have organised community groups in order to help relate their service more sensitively to local neighbourhood needs. Education departments have also been urged to relate their adult provision to local requirements and in various ways have adopted community education as their watchword. Still more generally, some more venturesome authorities are in the process of decentralising services to neighbourhood offices.

Regarded solely as a means of improving service delivery, these developments may mean little more, in community education for instance, than the dual use of school buildings and still more officers' meetings in which the local people, for whose benefit the changes have notionally been introduced, have no say. In such cases, the term 'community' has been misappropriated to give a pleasant gloss to what is little more than a bureaucratic re-organisation. On the other hand, these changes in service administration have often led to rather wider changes in practice in which partnerships have been established between the local authority, community groups and voluntary organisations. The residents' councils in Northampton, the community education forums in Tameside and the neighbourhood councils in Islington all illustrate the ways in which, up and down the country, changes in the administration of service provision are now trying actively to involve the local community in consultation, in planning and, in some measure, in controlling those services.

In our view, this more active involvement of local neighbourhoods is not only beneficial to those communities, it is equally valuable for the local authorities as well. However, it may well be that this account has so far taken too optimistic and too uncritical a view of the role of local authorities in community development. It should not be forgotten that the authorities that are working in this field are still in the minority, and that, even among those which replied to our inquiry, a good number defined the field very narrowly indeed. There are many problems and difficulties with which community development faces local authorities, which will be considered in chapter 8.

The foregoing analysis, furthermore, while it clarifies the various interpretations that local authorities give to the idea of community development, nevertheless has the disadvantage that it inevitably takes this activity rather out of context. The next four chapters aim to place community development practice back into the context of a small number of local authorities which, in our opinion, offer interesting and informative examples of what good community development practice amounts to. Though the choice of these authorities is bound to be somewhat arbitrary, they were selected because they are among those which interpret community development fairly broadly, as covering a number of departments, and which also have a clear idea of how socio-economic change relates to their work in this field. They were also chosen because, though with one exception, district authorities, they have very varied historical, socio-economic and administrative backgrounds.

In order of presentation, Crewe and Nantwich Borough and Cambridge City Councils are examples of two very different districts which have only recently started to work in community development. Thamesdown District Council, on the other hand, has had a long tradition of work of this kind. As the former municipal borough of Swindon, it has grown rapidly since the early 1950s, first under the Town Development Act of 1952, when community work of a fairly conventional kind was established, and more recently under the economic expansion which has taken place along the M4 motorway westward from London. In all these cases, reference is also made to relevant work being done by the adjacent county council, though the analysis is fuller in the case of Cambridgeshire which, since the 1920s, has been involved in community education through Henry Morris's pioneering work in setting up a network of village colleges throughout the county. Finally, an account is given of the community development work that is being done by Newcastle upon Tyne City Council, a metropolitan district with the full portfolio of statutory powers, whose interest in community development began just before the reorganisation of local government in 1974. These accounts were completed in the second half of 1987, but some more recent information has been incorporated in them since then.

4 Crewe and Nantwich: A Decisive Start

Crewe and Nantwich Borough is the southernmost of the eight district authorities which are covered by Cheshire County Council. Most of the borough lies immediately to the west of the M6 motorway just north of Stoke-on-Trent and is relatively sparsely populated. While the two town centres are about four miles apart, the two towns now form an almost continuous urban development. The total population of approximately 89,000 in 1950 rose to 96,300 by 1985, over 80 per cent of it located in the two main towns of Crewe and Nantwich and in their immediate environs. The total black population of the borough is estimated at about 3,000, mainly Afro-Caribbeans living in Crewe.

Crewe was founded in 1837 by the Grand Junction Railway Company; and it was at Crewe that the main lines from Liverpool, Manchester and Scotland in due course met. Throughout the nineteenth century and until the 1930s, Crewe was predominantly a railway town. Even by the mid-1930s, 10,000 people were still employed by the London Midland and Scottish Railway, 7,000 of them in the locomotive works. But by this time, Crewe's industrial base began to be diversified as other engineering firms, notably Rolls-Royce Car Division, became large employers, while clothing manufacture also became significant, accounting for 7 per cent of employment in 1953.

The 1970s and 1980s saw substantial changes in the pattern of employment in Crewe. Whereas, in 1953, nearly 60 per cent of employment had been in manufacturing, by 1981 this figure was down to 47 per cent. This was mainly due to the rapid run-down of employment in railway engineering, from 7,000 people in the

---

This chapter has been written by David Cliffe.

mid-1960s to 4,700 in 1981 and 4,000 in 1986. There was a further reduction to the workforce in 1988, and the engineering works have been put up for sale.

Nantwich is one of the Cheshire salt-towns based in the Dane and Weaver river basin, but salt has not been mined in or around the town since 1856. It is now predominantly a shopping town and rural service centre as well as a popular tourist centre, with many well-preserved Georgian and Tudor buildings. The main industry in the 1950s and 1960s was clothing manufacture but that declined rapidly in the 1970s so that, by 1981, only 22 per cent of employment in Nantwich was in manufacturing.

The unemployment rate for Crewe and Nantwich has, through most of the 1970s and 1980s, been about 2 per cent lower than the national average and significantly lower than that of the North West region. In April 1986, the rate was 11.7 per cent. That the district, with its overall dependence on engineering, has managed to maintain this relatively good position can be accounted for by a number of factors, some of which will be considered later. However, the district is not without its problems. In the mid-1980s, Cheshire County Council undertook a study of deprivation in the county, identifying the wards which had the highest level of what it called 'family stress'. Of the 30 wards scoring highest in the county, six were inner urban wards in Crewe.

Crewe and Nantwich Borough Council was formed when local government was reorganised in 1974. The amalgamation of two predominantly Conservative authorities (Nantwich Urban and Nantwich Rural District Councils) and the predominantly Labour-controlled Crewe Municipal Borough Council produced an authority which has been finely balanced politically, although the Labour Party just held the balance of power for most of the 1970s. In the local government elections of spring 1987, however, there was a marginal change as the Conservatives gained one seat from Labour. The composition of the council was then 27 Conservative, 24 Labour, 3 Liberal and 3 Social Democratic. Before these elections, the council voted not to increase the rates; but even with some unexpected non-rate or rate support grant income and using some money from the reserves, real cuts in spending still had to be made. One-third of the council stands for re-election each year. Some observers in the borough consider that this, and the fact that the political balance is so fine, account for the borough's reputation as a relatively low-spending authority, though one senior officer questioned the validity of that reputation on the grounds that the borough had never been afraid 'to take bold investment decisions where these were seen as being in the best interests of the future development and welfare of the area.'

In 1985, members of the council voted to restructure the departments and committees of the authority. A new chief executive was appointed whose initial responsibility was to see this restructuring through in order 'to direct more resources towards the provision of services'. To this end, a number of senior and middle management posts were abolished and the main services were brought together into one 'umbrella' department. Unlike some local authorities, reorganisation did not involve decentralising services, which was not thought necessary given that the local population is highly concentrated. By the beginning of 1986/87, accordingly, the borough's eight depart-

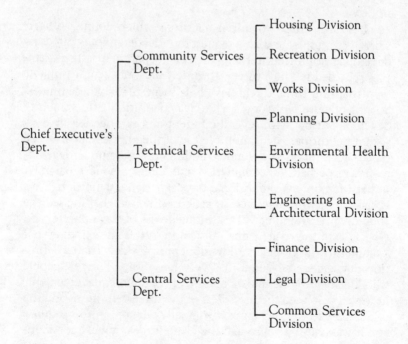

Figure 1 Crewe and Nantwich Borough Council – Pattern of Administration after Reorganisation, 1987

ments had been reduced to four: the Chief Executive's (which includes a Policy Development Division); the Community Services (including Housing, Recreation and Works); the Technical Services; and the Central Services Departments. In all, some 30 posts out of a total of 900 disappeared but some of these savings made it possible to establish new posts in front-line services. The consequences of this reorganisation (see Figure 1 above) for community development will be examined later on.

A policy for community development

Crewe and Nantwich Borough Council does not have a general policy for community development and the term seldom appears in its policy or policy-related documents. Given this lack of documentation, two questions immediately arose: first, why was the term not used and what implications did this have; and second, did the borough in fact undertake, or fund community development work under other guises and using different terminology.

These were the two initial questions which council officers were asked, together with a request for brief details of community development projects in their particular departments. The examples provided fell into three categories, most of them fitting two or perhaps all three categories. This suggests that these officers do not operate with one single clear definition of community development but with several different and not necessarily consistent definitions. This multiple use of the phrase appears to be based on common-sense understandings of 'community development', or perhaps of 'community' and 'development' separately, rather than on any professional or occupational definition. This is consistent with many recent articles which have criticised the wide-ranging and somewhat fashionable use of these phrases and especially of the term 'community', and with Cliffe's finding that 'community development' does not enjoy a widely shared definition but is generally used in a very loose way. The few people who did stick to one understanding of community development, however, also used the narrowest of the three definitions and the one closest to that which was originally adopted in this inquiry; and it was they who also had the clearest idea of what community development could achieve.

At its broadest, community development meant establishing or improving local authority services for the community generally or for individuals within the community. The examples given included introducing a radio-controlled telephone alarm scheme for the elderly and those with a handicap; introducing wheeled dustbins to improve refuse collection; and allowing concessionary access to municipal recreational facilities.

This broad use of the term focused on services generally and on the individual recipients of those services. But a narrower use of community development referred to services specifically to community groups. These examples included providing meeting spaces in community centres and halls; organising parent and toddler groups and play-groups; and providing facilities for sporting, cultural and recreational groups generally.

The narrowest usage of the term 'community development', however, shifted its focus significantly. For while the focus on community groups remained, the concern shifted from providing services *for* such groups to regarding them as considerably more than passive recipients of services. Community development in this usage involved encouraging community groups to form, supporting them once they had been established, enabling them to identify their own needs and priorities and providing resources, such as expert help, funding or premises so that those needs and priorities could be met. It was an important aspect of this approach to community development that the independence of these groups was recognised and that the contribution made by the local authority's staff should decrease as the groups became better able to manage their own affairs. Examples of community development using this approach included work with a variety of neighbourhood groups based in community centres; using an 'animateur' approach in recreation provision; and supporting tenants' and residents' associations and local economic development.

Several more general points about policy and community development emerged during interviews in the borough. One of the voluntary sector workers commented that since local government was re-organised in 1974, 'they [the local authority] are now starting to understand much better what community development work is and what it can achieve'. She was not clear whether these changes resulted directly from the fact that this re-organisation was intended to make services more responsive to the community or from the fact that senior officers have had more responsive and open attitudes, or whether it was because of changes in personnel in the senior and middle management of the authority. But whatever the cause, she was certain that the changes were real and positive.

One of the borough's senior officers, whose definition of 'community development' was similar to the advisory group's, suggested that the scope of community development work was very different in a county council compared with a district authority. Social services departments, for instance, have a tradition which is supported by legislation and which the district authorities do not share, of dealing more directly with issues like social and material deprivation, in relation to which a community development approach is often adopted. However, he accepted that this was not so much because district councils lacked the legislative framework for undertaking such work, but because its value was not recognised and because many district councils did not have the political will to provide resources for community development work. Another officer made the further point that community development did not only apply to recreational provision but was equally relevant to economic development and housing provision. As the next section shows, though most examples of community development work in Crewe and Nantwich were found in the Recreation Division, other departments had also begun to see its relevance and, in some cases, had begun to implement a community development policy.

In considering, first of all, examples of community development work which are consistent with the working party's definition, we do not wish to under-value work which is not included nor are we claiming that our use of the term is more valid than other usages. What we do hope to demonstrate, however, is that community development is based upon a clear and consistent set of principles which distinguish it from other work and that it has a unique and valuable contribution to make to the work of all tiers of local government.

The Chief Executive's Department

Since the authority was reorganised in 1985, the Chief Executive's Department has retained only a very limited role in the provision of direct services to the community. One of its major responsibilities, however, is policy development. The Policy Development Division has already undertaken a major review of economic development, which has implications for community development and a review of recreation provision was about to be started in which the role of community development in the borough's recreation strategy would be considered. The most significant field of community development work in the Chief Executive's Department, however, is that of employment and economic development. Over a long period, the area has had to cope with a steady decline in its traditional industrial base and, in particular, with the decline in the number of jobs in railway engineering. The borough's economic and employment strategy has several elements, some of which are carried out in co-operation with Cheshire County Council and other regional bodies. These include developing infrastructure and business parks, including ensuring that land is available; promoting the area to attract new businesses and industry; liaising with existing industry; promoting tourism; and supporting small businesses, new enterprises, and the local workforce. It is in these last two areas that the borough adopts a community development approach.

The Economic Policy Review argued that a strategy was needed to deal with pockets of very high unemployment among certain age groups in the borough. It noted that in 1983 a working party had been set up by the National Council for Voluntary Organisations (NCVO) and the local authority associations to assess the role of voluntary organisations in local economic development and remarked that

the Council does not appear to have significant contact with voluntary and community groups active in creating jobs and identifying local economic needs. What is needed is to bring together officers and members and voluntary/community organisations to discuss effective ways of working together to help the unemployed and stimulate community enterprise.

As a first step, it proposed to hold a local seminar on this topic, with a development officer from NCVO as advisor.

Another aspect of community development policy is the support that is offered to unemployed people under a modest but important loan guarantee scheme. Under the Government's Enterprise Allowance Scheme, grants are available to help unemployed people start up their own businesses. The council has recognised that some people are unable to raise the £1,000 necessary to qualify for the Scheme and has offered to guarantee such loans so as to enable some unemployed people to take advantage of it. The borough also contributes to community development through grant aid. In 1986/7, grant aid to voluntary organisations (including the local voluntary service council) amounted to £38,000. Other grant aid is made available through budgets administered by the Community Services Department. The Chief Executive's Department could make a contribution to community development by using the Manpower Services Commission's Community Programme. So far, the borough has only used the programme for small projects like helping elderly people to maintain their gardens but it is now investigating the possibility of doing so for projects 'in areas such as environmental improvement, tourism development, amenity provision and local welfare assistance'. Though it is possible to adopt a community development approach in some of these areas, there are many who doubt what can be achieved using this source of funding because of the conditions which are attached to it, not least the time limits on the periods of employment. No one in the Chief Executive's Department is responsible for community development initiatives in the department, but if the plans for stimulating community enterprise in the field of employment mature, any staff involved would have clear community development responsibilities.

The Community Services Department
The Community Services Department comprises the council's main services separated into three divisions, Housing, Recreation and Works. It was in the first two divisions that examples of community development, as the advisory group defined it, were found. As well as staff who are based in the administrative divisions, the department has a small central administrative and support unit. In the structure proposed for the department, one of the posts in this unit is that of Playleader/Community Worker to assist 'in the organisation of playschemes, activities, events and departmental promotions including those in Council owned community facilities in sheltered units'. This post could clearly stimulate a wide range of community development initiatives throughout the department, but the council had not found funding for it.

The Housing Division
No staff in the Housing Division had any significant responsibility for community development as the advisory group defined it. The division's approach to community development was mainly to encourage voluntary organisations and community groups involved in community development initiatives, and to

offer them help in kind, especially by making premises available and involving staff from other divisions in the department, especially the Recreation Division. Such cross-divisional co-operation is facilitated by the new structure of the department. In other cases, contributions are made by staff from outside the authority, notably from Cheshire County Council Social Services Department and voluntary organisations.

Among the initiatives in which the Housing Division is in-volved are the following. The County Council has identified several areas of high 'family stress' within Crewe, in two of which the division has supported community development initiatives. The Moat House Drive Family Centre, for example, is based in a flat which is rent- and rate-free and whose costs are also covered by the division. It is run by a local voluntary management committee on which sit local authority representatives. Activi-ties in the centre are initiated and managed locally and include a parent and toddler group, welfare rights and other advice sessions and events organised by the Pre-School Playgroups Association. Small sums of money to support these activities have been made available by the Social Services Department and the Govern-ment's Opportunities for Volunteering Scheme.

A similar but larger project was set up in the St Barnabas area of Crewe. The Our House project is based in two council houses which are provided rent- and rate-free and with overheads covered by the division. However, unlike the Moat House Cen-tre, Our House also serves as a base for a full-time community worker employed by the Social Services Department, with whose support a number of local community groups and initiatives have been organised. Our House is also a base for a local housing office where residents can easily contact housing staff who can deal immediately with any housing problems.

In recent years, the Housing Division has been identifying and declaring General Improvement Areas (GIAs). In the last five of these GIAs, it has encouraged local communities to set up residents' associations, for which it at first also provided clerical support. The associations have mainly helped the division by providing forums for consultation on the environmental and other issues which arise in GIA improvement schemes. However, once established, these residents' associations could clearly deal with much wider questions than these, though whether any of them have developed this wider role is not known.

The Housing Division also supports tenants' associations in areas with large numbers of council properties, generally by making premises available to them as meeting places and activity centres. Tenants' associations in the borough tend to wax and wane in their levels of activity and from time to time they collapse altogether. This happened to one association on the Moat House estate, and the flat they had used was then returned to the housing stock.

These fluctuations in both tenants' and residents' associations are found in many other areas and are common to many voluntary groups which have no paid staff to ensure their continuity. The Council, and in particular the Housing Division, might well consider following the example of other authorities by appointing an officer with a specific responsibility for working with these local associations. The officer's brief may simply be to enable associations to keep going through periods of crisis, perhaps by helping them to recruit new members and by recognising the valuable complementary role which they can play in housing administration. But the brief may be much wider and could recognise the contribution which neighbourhood organisations can make to issues other than housing. Here the officer does not simply support ailing associations but adopts a community development approach in helping these local community groups to identify their own needs and priorities and to find ways of meeting them.

Finally, the division has promoted community development work by opening up the communal lounges of the borough's 12 sheltered housing schemes. As local community facilities are scarce in many parts of the borough, this policy makes a valuable resource available to the community generally, while bringing the residents of the sheltered housing schemes into contact with the wider community. Among the projects developed in these communal lounges have been luncheon clubs, whose equipment, heating and lighting costs are covered by the Housing Division; day care centres, with these costs covered jointly with the Social Services Department, which also employs the staff and recruits volunteer helpers; and some dance and art ventures with staff employed by the Recreation Division.

The Recreation Division

Nowhere in the draft report on the development of the borough's recreation plan does the phrase 'community development' appear. Its focus is upon the direct provision of recreation services and upon co-ordinating recreation provision in the voluntary and private sectors. This approach is typical of the traditional practice of recreation departments. However, one senior recreation officer said that 'the facility boom is over. We are past the period of expansion of recreation resources and into the period when we need to develop and expand community use. We need to enable people to help themselves.' In using sports and arts as a means to community development, he thought it was necessary first of all to identify under-used facilities such as village and school halls, the communal lounges of housing developments and spaces in factories, which could be used in isolated and often badly-served communities. The next step was to put on attractive programmes, artistic, cultural, sporting and recreational, with skilled staff to stimulate community involvement in them. However, one of their aims would be to enable these communities to develop into cohesive groups with common interests and practical skills so that the staff could eventually be reduced or withdrawn altogether. Such an approach, this worker continued, would not only provide a service where there had been none before, making efficient use of limited resources, but would also engage the potential of local communities themselves. It was widely expected that the forthcoming recreation plan would endorse this community development approach. However, there are some obstacles that have to be faced, of which the most significant is the fact that recreation facilities, such as community and sports centres, are run as 'cost-centres'. As a recent paper states, 'The object of the [Recreation] Division is to continue the development of opportunities for the enjoyment of sport, leisure time and promotion of the Arts *and to maximise* the full potential of facility usage and *income operation* [our italics].' Community development projects in the field of recreation which do not involve large numbers of people or generate much income are not going to be easy to bring into line with this objective. However, the Recreation Division remains the main agency for community development work in the borough and some of the following examples have already begun to adopt this new approach.

The Recreation Division employs one full-time senior officer with the title community development officer. Before the council's departments were reorganised, he was one of the three managers of the impressive Victoria Community Centre and Community School in the town centre. When the Recreation Division was created, the opportunity was taken to re-assess the role of a number of posts, including that of the community development officer himself. As he had been mainly responsible for running the Victoria Centre, and as the centre had become well established, his job description was changed so as to remove most of his management responsibilities and release him to work on the 'provision of a Recreation Plan . . . and to develop links with the community outside the Victoria Centre on a much broader basis . . .' Although these changes were adopted, they were not put into effect because, at the end of 1986, the officer was made responsible for planning and setting up the Crewe Heritage Festival. However, by late summer of 1987, he was expected to be free to resume his new role, in which he will be responsible for working out the division's community development policy.

The Victoria Centre is a large building near the centre of Crewe. It was mainly financed by the county council, the borough, the Department of Education and the Sports Council and took from the late 1970s until 1982 to complete. The Community School is located on two sites, with a lower school for 11–13 year olds, based on the original Ludford Street Junior School, and an upper school using three new purpose-built centres. As an article in the *Architects' Journal* noted, 'Community use includes adult education courses, sports facilities for individuals, lettings to local groups and societies, PTA meetings, private functions and the borough's leisure department's own promotions.' Most of these uses are relatively formal, timetabled and operate to clear financial targets, users being attracted to the centre from all over the town and further afield.

While the staff on the 'community' side of the Victoria Centre are employed by the Recreation Division, they are jointly financed by the borough and the county council. Links with staff on the 'school' side are limited, since the school has no trained community teachers. By contrast, most of the 'community' provision on the Ludford site is designed for and used by people from the immediate neighbourhood. One member of the 'community' staff is mainly based in Ludford and she, as the family centre organiser, adopts a primarily community development approach. She is involved in initiating and developing a range of activities for community groups in the neighbourhood in which the Victoria Centre is located; for parent and toddler groups, playgroups, a residents' association, a slimming circle, a Gingerbread group, and a range of activities for pensioners. Most of this work is done from a community centre but, like most workers who operate from a building, the organiser also has financial and administrative responsibilities which limit the amount and kind of community work which she can do.

Staff in the Victoria Centre are also responsible for promoting outreach work across the entire borough. One piece of work was regarded as having been particularly significant in getting a community development approach to recreation provision adopted. In 1986, with funding from a number of sources including the borough council, the county council, the Cheshire Dance Workshop, the Gulbenkian Foundation and the North West Arts Association, the borough made use of a dance animateur employed by the Cheshire Dance Workshop. An animateur approach was adopted because to have employed one person as a traditional tutor would have limited the number of groups which could be supported. The intention was to provide a short-term stimulus to new or existing community groups, in such a way that they could continue to function independently after the professional worker was withdrawn. Working with community associations and mother and toddler groups in village halls, with groups of elderly people in the community lounges of sheltered housing schemes and with other groups, both the person who was appointed and the approach adopted justified the initial hopes. This helped to generate proposals for a permanent post to be established, using a similar approach, which is described below.

A new community hall attached to the Civic Hall in Nantwich town centre was opened in 1987. A new post of outreach worker has also been under discussion. Although based at the new community hall, this worker would mostly work outside the building with relatively isolated communities in a way similar to that of the dance animateur. Although a detailed programme of work for this new post was still to be worked out, the general approach was clear.

The other way in which the Recreation Division facilitates community development is through grant aid. Small grants are available from a general fund, larger grants by separate committee decision. The annual budget of £16,000 for small grant-aided schemes is split into grants that are made to parish councils to provide village halls and playing fields and grants to voluntary, adult sports and cultural organisations. This grant aid contributes to community development throughout the borough either by helping to provide facilities for community groups to use or by providing small sums to cover some of the running costs of a number of voluntary organisations. The grant-aid budget has not been increased for a number of years despite the fact that new initiatives have stimulated more community groups to ask for grants. The possibility of reorganising, and possibly increasing the size of the grant-aid budget is currently being considered.

Play schemes and play leadership are separately funded with a budget in 1986/87 of £3,400. This is used to employ a number of play leaders and to meet the running costs of council and voluntary play schemes. Without these small sums most of these schemes could not run. However, the potential for promoting a wider programme of community development work which would make use of these communities' commitment to play is not being exploited by the borough, nor has it the staff to build upon these opportunities.

The Community Services Committee also makes additional grants to voluntary organisations. Two projects funded in recent years have a community development role. The Camm Street gymnasium and Community Centre is based in one of Crewe's inner urban wards. In 1980/81, with the borough's support, it obtained an Urban Programme grant to enable it to convert an old factory and to cover some of its running costs for five years. The project was initiated by the local community and is now run by a voluntary management committee. It aims first of all to provide a well-equipped gymnasium, and subsequently a community centre to serve the neighbourhood. Though by 1986/87 the Urban Programme funding for the project had ended, the borough council agreed to contribute £5,000 a year for a further five years to help cover the running costs, in the expectation that, at the end of that period, the project would be self-financing. How far the community centre was meeting the needs of the immediate neighbourhood was questionable. Certainly, some local people used it, but people came to the gymnasium from all parts of the borough and it was clear that not all the local groups saw the Camm Street centre as adequate since they were putting pressure on the Recreation Division to provide another community centre, especially for the local black population, which is a sizeable group in this part of the town.

The Crewe Alexandra Soccer Skills and Community Centre Project is a more recent initiative to which the borough council is contributing £9,000 a year. Sports Council and other money has been put into this venture, which aims to provide both improved facilities for the local football club and new facilities for the community. As this is a relatively new project, it is still unclear how much more than an additional sports facility it will become.

Cheshire County Council's role

In interviewing borough council officers, the general point was made that when community development projects are initiated by local government departments or voluntary organisations funded by local authorities, the traditional barriers between departments rapidly and, it seems, almost inevitably become blurred. For instance, an officer of the Recreation Division working with a neighbourhood group is as likely to be dealing with issues related to housing provision or welfare rights as to be working solely in the recreation field. But while consultation between different departments and different tiers of local government is desirable, it is not easily achieved, so that arrangements for the joint funding of community development work, for example, have to be made *ad hoc* since the structures for such discussions do not exist. As a result, community development is under-funded because it is unclear whose responsibility it is and its potential is accordingly under-valued. The county council's main opportunities for doing community development are in the fields of education and social services.

The Education Department

The county's Education Department does not have a tradition of community education. Its schools have primarily operated as conventional educational institutions, with the Victoria Centre one of the few exceptions. Nor has the further education sector been particularly concerned with community activities, while the adult education service, at least in Crewe and Nantwich, has mainly provided a very traditional programme of classes. One staff member in the local college of further education did appear to have some responsibility for outreach work, and some school heads have made their premises available for use both by the community and by workers from other departments, including the Recreation Division. It is hoped that this practice will grow, particularly in the villages, where the school is often the only public building. Recent staff changes in the Education Department make it more likely that this hope may be fulfilled, if only slowly. The Education Department has also created the new post of joint use liaison officer, whose brief is to identify the wider uses to which education premises can be put. However, given the practical problems, such as making school buildings suitable for community use, changing caretaking patterns, and the possible reluctance of some heads, with their traditional professional autonomy, to collaborate, it is not expected that joint use will develop very speedily.

The Social Services Department

Most of the area covered by the borough falls within one of the county council's Social Services Department's districts. Though one of the seven social work teams in the district is called the Community Services Team, only a limited amount of its work can be described as community development. It deals with services like home-helps and day-care provision for the frail elderly.

The Team also organises neighbourhood visiting and befriending schemes which have some potential for community development. Funding is available for part-time staff to set up and support these schemes, some of which also operate in the rural parts of the borough.

The department's most significant contribution to community development, however, is through two full-time posts within the Community Services Team. One of these is the community worker at the Our House project in Crewe, which is run jointly with the Housing Division, and the other is a community social worker. This post, which is not neighbourhood-based, involves helping to initiate and support developments in the voluntary sector. Most of the work is done in Crewe but some rural work has also been carried out recently, including setting up Bunbury Community Care, a good neighbour scheme based in a parish with a population of about 1,200. Both of these posts were established as a result of the County Council's identification of areas of high 'family stress' in some of the inner areas of Crewe.

The voluntary sector

The voluntary sector in Crewe and Nantwich has not traditionally been very strong. Since its creation in the mid-nineteenth and well into the twentieth century, Crewe was a company-town for British Rail and its predecessors, including the London and North-Western Railway. The company provided health and welfare services for its employees and their families, a benign paternalism which inhibited the development of a vigorous tradition of self-help or organisation in the local communities. This helps to account for the relative weakness of the local voluntary sector and the difficulties which activists have experienced in organising community action. This is compounded by the local authorities' attitude to the voluntary sector for, in line with the town's paternalistic ethos, councillors and officers of the local authorities have until quite recently failed to recognise the need for and potential of the voluntary sector which has been supported parsimoniously.

These attitudes have changed in recent years. As Crewe has become less of a railway town and as its economic base has diversified, so the old paternalism has declined and the voluntary sector has burgeoned. The borough council, accordingly, through both the Community Services and the Chief Executive's Departments, has funded a number of voluntary sector initiatives, some in the community development field, thus recognising the role which the voluntary sector can play in the borough's social development. This change has taken place since the new Chief Executive was appointed and the Council's services reorganised. Among the voluntary projects funded are the Council for Voluntary Services, the Camm Street Project and the Crewe Alexandra Soccer Skills Scheme. Many of them have only been partly funded by the Borough Council, with the balance coming from other sources, including the Urban Programme and the County Council.

The voluntary sector, however, still faces funding problems since the Community Services Department's grant-aid budget is small and has not increased for several years. The Council is to review the size and purpose of this budget. Another problem which is also being considered is that grant aid is allocated for a limited period of time. The County and Borough Councils are presently discussing the possibility of jointly providing core-funding for several major voluntary organisations, one of the most important of which is the Council for Voluntary Service.

The CVS is a small organisation which employs only three full time staff, including a general secretary and a volunteer organiser. Until 1986, it was funded from a number of relatively short-term sources, such as Opportunities for Volunteering and the Community Programme, which the Social Services Department supplemented with a grant of a few thousand pounds. In late 1985, however, the Borough Council agreed to support a bid by the CVS for an Urban Aid grant. This was the last year in which authorities like the Borough Council were eligible to apply for Urban Aid. The bid, which was successful, has paid for a new centre for the CVS and some of its salary costs. Most local voluntary organisations are affiliated to the CVS, which provides them with information and practical support as well as representing them on various local bodies. The general secretary of the CVS sees one of her roles as being to encourage the local authorities to appreciate the positive role which the voluntary sector has to play and to develop policies and provide support to enable it to fulfil that role.

Parish councils
Only 20 per cent of the borough's inhabitants live outside the towns of Crewe and Nantwich. This rural area is covered by over 60 parishes, only 16 of which have populations of more than

300, and the largest a population of only about 1,600. Some of the villages have a village hall or some other meeting place, but the parishes' rate-income is not sufficient for them to employ staff of their own. The Community Services Department has recognised that, although most people in the rural areas are mobile, there is a sizeable minority which is not. Some of its recent initiatives, accordingly, such as the work of the dance animateur and other outreach staff, have begun to deal with their specific needs. The rural populations are too small and too dispersed, however, to justify any large capital investment but, by using parish council buildings, useful work can still be done. A community development approach is essential since it allows outreach staff to withdraw, or at least reduce their commitment at some point so that staff can be redirected to work in other areas and it is expected that this approach to work with rural communities will be incorporated into the forthcoming Recreation Plan.

Summing up

In the last few years, Crewe and Nantwich Borough Council has begun to see the advantages of a community development approach to providing services and in its work with local communities, whether carried out directly or through the voluntary sector. This new awareness has been particularly noticeable since the borough's administration was reorganised. It has informed the recent Economic Development Policy Review as well as the thinking which has gone into the review of recreation policy and rural community development. At the same time, the Council has begun more clearly to understand the important role of the voluntary sector in complementing the local authority's own services. Consequently, it has begun to increase funding for the voluntary sector and is at present reviewing some of its policies towards it.

One obstacle in the way of developing clear and well considered policies for community development, however, lies in the wide and differing understandings of the term 'community development'. Only a few Borough Council officers use the phrase as it was originally used by the advisory group. What the other officers miss are the unique features of community development which make it valuable as an approach and which distinguish it from other kinds of work. More than one person commented that this report would be particularly useful if it could spell out, and illustrate with good examples, exactly what is special about community development and what it can achieve in local government work.

Community development initiatives tend very quickly to cross the traditional boundaries of local authority departments. For that reason, joint funding both between different tiers of local authorities and between them and other agencies, such as arts associations or the Sports Council, however desirable, is often difficult to achieve since structures for setting it up do not exist. Consequently, community development projects are either not funded or are funded on insecure short-term contracts because not all of the parties involved are able or willing to fund them permanently. Partly for these reasons, district authorities such as Crewe and Nantwich are hesitant to commit funds to community development projects, especially if their focus may shift from, say, recreation provision, for which the borough is responsible, to activities which are seen as being closer to the personal social services, which are the County's responsibility. Local authorities have been more willing to make such commitments when external sources of funding, such as the Urban Programme, have been available. Borough Council officers now anticipate that, without this source of funding, which was withdrawn from most local authorities in 1985, decisions about whether or not to fund community development projects will be much more difficult. New structures for inter-agency funding of community development projects would increase both the number and the security of such projects.

5 Cambridge and Cambridgeshire: Tradition and Innovation

Cambridge City Council

Cambridge is best known for its university which has developed over the past eight centuries. The mediaeval town centre is encircled by the university colleges, and the River Cam and a ring of commons and open spaces make a clear division between this central area and the suburbs. The suburbs themselves vary greatly. Long avenues of large, detached houses mark the middle class districts of the city, particularly in the south, while late nineteenth century brick terraces dominate the working class districts which followed the railway development in the east. In the north, there are a number of large council estates, some the cottage-terrace type of the interwar period, the rest of the 'Cambridge brick' post-war variety.

The university brings Cambridge its wealth. Not only is employment generated by the colleges, but the scientific research carried out there has attracted high-technology industry to the town. Over two hundred such firms have been established in and around the city, in what has been called the 'Cambridge phenomenon'. The charm of the university buildings and grounds also attracts large numbers of tourists. Over 3 million people visit Cambridge each year, spending £110 million and making it one of Britain's top five tourist attractions. Finally, Cambridge is a regional service centre: reaching out to north Suffolk and south Cambridgeshire, the city has a catchment area of around 400,000 people whom it attracts with its good range of shops. Many regional businesses are based in the city, as are the county council offices. All this activity has kept unemployment in Cambridge at the relatively low level of 6.8 per cent.

This chapter has been written by Rodney Hedley.

The city's affluence hits the observer. But the affluence hides problems. There are certainly jobs to be had, but the growth industries want skilled and educated workers who come from outside the city. A buoyant job market for the middle class has raised house prices, which throughout the town are high, and has begun to put pressure on the surrounding villages. Tourists also force up prices so that the cost of living is equally high. The university provides many service jobs, most of them low-paid. There is, therefore, a division between the 'centre and rest', a modern form of 'town and gown' perhaps, and city councillors and officers are keen to try to redistribute resources away from the college ring. While in Parliamentary representation the city is staunchly Conservative, the city council is hung, Labour having 22 seats and the Conservatives and Alliance 11 each.

In 1985/86, Cambridge City spent around £30 million on its services, of which the Community Services budget was £460,000, including grants to voluntary organisations. Rates have risen over the last five years as the Labour administration has taken on new commitments. As the city council's annual report states, 'The Council continues to give overriding emphasis to its policies for housing, employment generation and protection, community welfare and development and the pursuit of peace.'

Early approaches to community development
Until 1982, the city council's approach to community initiatives, apart from providing sports and recreation facilities, was piecemeal. The Amenities and Recreation Department provided resources for summer play schemes, grant aided a number of voluntary groups, and was responsible for part-financing community centre facilities in the county council's community schools. At the time, it was generally held that the county had the expertise to stimulate group activity, while the city's role was limited to finance.

New approaches first appeared in the Housing Department. In the mid-1970s, several areas were designated for housing improvement and a General Improvement Area Team and a Housing Estates Project were set up. To implement the renovation programmes required consultation. This had traditionally meant, as one commentator put it, 'tenant to council; council to decide'. However, mostly due to the efforts of one officer, the teams encouraged residents' associations to be formed, while existing ones were strengthened to facilitate the consultation process. As a representative from the housing team said,

At first this approach felt very threatening to council officers and councillors alike. For council officers it was as if their professional skill was being undermined; and for councillors the fear was that they would simply not be needed. In fact the outcome proved the opposite. Officers had greater opportunity to use their skills, and the councillors saw their status and prestige raised. The whole consultation process was, and is, more meaningful and cost effective.

The benefits were quickly obvious as residents' views on building design and the provision of open spaces were accepted: and one tenants' hall and play area has recently received an RIBA award. Indeed, the Housing Department has continued to recognise and support residents' and tenants' associations, for which a senior officer is now responsible. An organisational structure has also been set up, with teams of officers working in areas coterminous with wards, and housing assistants employed to work with community groups and to associate them with the initiatives taken by the Community Services Team which was to be set up.

A plan for community development, 1982–85
The move to set up a special unit to deal with community development did not come until 1982, when the city council launched its community and welfare initiative. This brainchild of the Labour administration was promoted by a councillor who worked in Harlow, where he was impressed by the council's community development approach. Although sponsored by Labour, the plan seems to have been genuinely supported by all political parties, which made it very much easier for the staff to carry out. The initiative was overseen by a Community Services panel, a working party of councillors, and a review of community provision was carried out by an officer from the Planning Department, who had to draw up a neighbourhood analysis of the city and produce data on disadvantaged groups. At the end of 1983, a co-ordinator was appointed to see the plan through.

The Community Welfare and Development Plan was published in October 1985 and subsequently approved by the council. It spelt out what Cambridge City Council saw as community development. It was a process which aimed (a) to increase people's ability to act together to increase their influence and control, (b) to develop their skills, knowledge, experience and confidence, and (c) to discriminate positively in favour of those least able to articulate their needs and help themselves. Consistent with these aims was the decision to adopt a community work approach to strengthen local communities, to encourage the relevant community resource agencies to co-operate and, most important for the evaluation of the policy, to accept that community development was a gradual process.

The plan envisaged that a Community Services Team would be established with responsibility for community work in neighbourhoods and throughout the City. The organisation of the team is shown in Figure 2. It is one section among three within the Amenities and Recreation Department (the other sections being Recreation and Parks and Entertainments and Tourism), and is answerable to the Community Services Committee. The team is led by an assistant amenities and recreation officer (community services), who is accountable to the amenities and recreation officer himself. Selecting the right manager for the team was very important since he or she not only had to have considerable community work experience to be able to implement the plan but also had to 'sell' the idea to a wide range of agencies. Managerial skills were therefore crucial; and the chair of community services considered that much of the team's success was a result of this good appointment.

In the Community Welfare and Development Plan, the city, which has a population of 99,000, was divided into 59 neighbourhoods, each with a population of between 1,500 to 3,000. The plan envisaged community development officers, with clerical assistants, being based in a number of these neighbourhoods where they would stimulate community activity. Neighbourhoods were to be chosen according to socio-economic criteria and existing community resources. Neighbourhood bases were essential for their work. The most established community centre network in the city were the county council's community primary schools, which the city partly financed, so it was decided to introduce community workers into these schools. Following negotiations with the county, these officers have been appointed. Furthermore, in two cases where the schools did not have adequate community facilities, the district financed the building of additional halls. Community shops and houses, as well as schools, have been provided as neighbourhood bases to be shared by all the community services, the Housing Department and voluntary organisations.

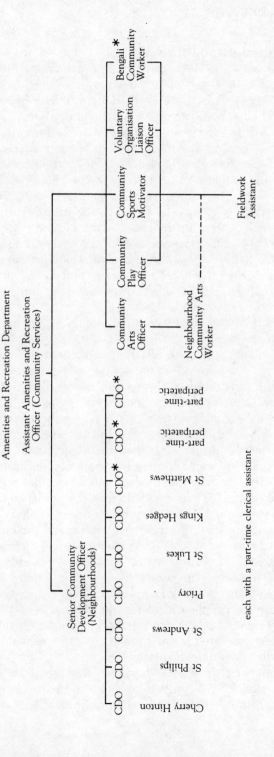

Figure 2 Cambridge City Council – Community Services Team, May 1987.

Issues in neighbourhood provision

How this works out in practice can be illustrated from three neighbourhoods in the north of the town which cover large council estates: Abbey, Arbury and East Chesterton. The Abbey and Arbury neighbourhoods each have a community house. In Abbey, this is used by the Housing Department as an informal drop-in and advice centre; in Arbury, the house was pioneered by the Save the Children Fund and is used for more intensive support work with families. Arbury also has a community shop which is jointly used by Community Services and Housing for advising and supporting groups. In addition, sheltered housing was used as resource centres for the East Chesterton and Abbey neighbourhoods. In East Chesterton, most of the work was done in the purpose-built primary school and halls were also being added to the schools in the other two areas: at St Luke's, for example, the council spent £180,000 on a 'Swedest' purpose-built hall.

Working from their community centre bases, the community development officers were responsible for maintaining and developing a large number of centre activities, which ranged from bridge and women's self-defence to model car racing and pensioner clubs. Although based in centres, all the workers were committed to working in the neighbourhoods so as to link facilities, such as the community shop, the house and church halls, together. However, this outreach approach posed managerial problems, as the people who used the centres still saw community development staff as primarily responsible for organising centre activities, so that staff tended to be bogged down in work within the centres. A report by Peterborough on its community services had noted that community workers tended to become simply booking-clerks for centre activities; and the city council had tried to forestall this danger by providing clerical staff to help with the administration of the centres. Nevertheless, in the purpose-built community school of St Andrew's, which had been a highly successful community facility since the mid-1970s, the local people considered that the role of the community development officer was primarily to encourage the existing community activities within the school's catchment area rather than in the wider neighbourhood.

How successful, then, are these educational establishments in pioneering community development? Schools, and particularly primary schools, certainly help to give their neighbourhoods an identity. But most areas are still defined by the names of their schools rather than by those of the neighbourhoods: a small point perhaps, but facilities must serve their neighbourhoods, not neighbourhoods the facilities. Nevertheless, in all three neighbourhoods the various agencies worked together very successfully – the Housing Department, the Save the Children Fund Project and the County Education Service, although health and social services were less in evidence.

The officer who managed the neighbourhood work said that outreach work was a priority and that one advantage of working in a team was that workers did not become isolated and could learn from each other about different methods of neighbourhood work. Furthermore, most community development officers had only been in post for less than a year, so that they were new to the work. He also expected some of the schools to change once the re-organisation of the Community Education Service had become fully effective, when all Cambridge's community schools and institutions would be grouped together in 'patches', which would be expected to adopt a neighbourhood approach.

The experience of neighbourhood work had led to the Community Welfare and Development Plan being revised. The 59 neighbourhoods are considered to be too small, so they have now been grouped together into clusters with populations of between 7,000 and 10,000, roughly equivalent to the size of an electoral ward. One advantage of this revision is that these wider areas correspond with those of the Housing Department. Finally, the neighbourhoods have been grouped into two categories according to their needs: the 'A' type, where a full-time community development worker and supporting staff needs to be based in the area, and the 'B' type, where the needs are not so great and where part-time peripatetic community workers can be employed.

City-wide initiatives

The team's city-wide brief involves specialist workers stimulating projects which have a significance for the community as a whole and take account of special needs and disadvantages. These workers deal with grants, community arts and play.

The council's grants budget has grown considerably since the Community Services Team was set up. In 1986/87, it was £200,000, which was just under half of the Community Services' budget. Grant aid is given to organisations dealing with the under-fives, children's play facilities and family support and young people; with ethnic minorities, elderly people, unemployed people and women; people with disabilities and single parents; city resource, advice centres and community associations. In addition to this fund, small grants are allocated from the council's lottery. The officer responsible for grant aid also has a small budget for training in voluntary groups. Several community development projects for the unemployed and the Save the Children Fund have also been given grants to enable them to employ development officers. Neighbourhood groups requiring money may also approach the team. The Arbury Residents' Association, for example, had received £3,000 but it is recognised that, as neighbourhood groups' demands grow, it may be sensible to allocate grant aid specifically to the neighbourhoods.

The community arts officer is responsible for promoting arts in the city and the neighbourhoods, in which she is assisted by a neighbourhood community arts officer who is partly funded by the Eastern Arts Council. These officers think of arts activities as tools in community development; community arts means more than encouraging people to join in a street festival once a year or measuring success by the number of amateur dramatics societies that were started. So, as well as organising larger events, the neighbourhood arts officer works in a neighbourhood, helping local groups to develop their self-expression and understanding. The arts officers said that their work fits well into that of the Community Services Team and that it is helped, for example, by the fact that the neighbourhood arts officer works alongside community development officers in the neighbourhoods. Community development required a gradual approach, and this allowed it; too often arts officers were parachuted into areas to organise a festival, only to disappear when it was over.

The play worker had previously organised her work in another section of the Amenities Department. She is not fully convinced of the wisdom of placing play in the Community Service's Team, since most of the work still involves other sections of the Amenities Department. She sees play more as a matter of providing a direct service than as a community development process. The budget for play schemes – around £4,000 – was fairly large.

Evaluation

For Cambridge City, community development is about people organising their own projects so as to gain more influence and control, and discriminating in favour of the disadvantaged. The city council has now created a framework, both in the neighbourhoods and throughout the city, for helping people to organise their own projects. In the absence of survey material, we can only rely on the impressions of people who actually used the centres, though these were likely to be favourable. In the neighbourhood projects, most people said that the city council's new approach was good, partly because their neighbourhoods were getting the attention and resources they did not have before and partly because it seemed easier compared with the arrangements which the county council had previously made. Certainly, the number and variety of activities was most impressive. There was also a distinct feeling of optimism about what was going on in the neighbourhoods.

From the point of view of the voluntary organisations, the council's new approach seemed to be more effective in helping to start projects and schemes and keep them going. Phrases like 'we know where to go now', 'we can sound out ideas', 'we can see our work in relation to others', were frequently used. The team has also done a valuable job in getting 'community services' accepted as a legitimate function of the city council; while having a specialist Community Services Committee was regarded as especially helpful since 'provision has to be debated fully by councillors now and measures don't disappear into other committees'. Thus, it was clear that Community Services was highly regarded and had succeeded in making community development intelligible and accepted. County officers, for example, said that they had learnt much from the Cambridge City Team, and that the team had helped to achieve a consensus about what community development meant. As a result, as one officer put it, 'When agencies meet we don't argue about the nature of community development, it is accepted. We talk about getting on with the job.'

The voluntary organisations accordingly feel that they now have more of a say in the city's community work in the neighbourhoods and there are many associations whose membership had gone up and where the attendance at meetings had increased. The Housing Department's decentralised operation makes it easier for it to assess how its policy is working out and, with the dovetailing of community services, the city administration as a whole is moving towards a more decentralised system. Indeed, the chair of the Community Services Committee considered the team to be 'paving the way for the decentralisation of all council services'. Decentralisation was intended not only to make services more accountable, and thereby more effective, but to redistribute resources to the suburbs, which had been neglected, particularly in the arts. Councillors also commented that their role as representatives had been enhanced by the neighbourhood approach since they knew more about what was going on in their wards.

Increasing their influence and control is particularly important to the disadvantaged. The designation of priority neighbourhoods was based on an analysis of need, using indicators like the percentage of unemployment, overcrowding and the absence of amenities. The neighbourhood approach and the council's policy on grant applications have maintained a commitment to these groups. Difficult though this is to quantify, the growing numbers of self-help groups in these categories and the fact that voluntary effort has been redirected in their favour suggest that the community development policy is succeeding in discriminating positively in favour of the disadvantaged. More generally, the city's community development policy appears to have resulted in very real gains and the model which has been adopted may well be one which many districts may wish to consider.

Cambridgeshire County Council

Cambridgeshire was formed in 1974 by the amalgamation of the two counties of Cambridgeshire and the Isle of Ely together with Huntingdon and Peterborough. It has a population of around 620,000. The county is predominantly rural with a highly dispersed population, and Peterborough and Cambridge are the two main urban centres.

Cambridgeshire is also a prosperous county. Unemployment is less than 6 per cent overall, though it ranges from 2.5 per cent in Huntingdon to 11.5 in Wisbech. The area's economic buoyancy is due to the expansion of light industry based on the new technologies, many pioneered in Cambridgeshire, and the steady industrial growth in Peterborough and the Ouse Valley, which includes Huntingdon and St Neots. Agriculture – arable farming and market gardening – is important but it employs only 5 per cent of the county's work-force. In the last 10 years, the county's population has increased by 13 per cent because of the development of Peterborough as an expanding town and the generally favourable economic climate.

County authorities are responsible for education, social services, the police, public protection (including fire services), libraries and museums, transportation, probation and planning. Cambridgeshire spends about £290 millions on these services. As in other county councils, the largest single item of expenditure is education, which takes 60 per cent of the county budget. The rapid population growth in the county has put much pressure on its finances so that, over the last 10 years, its budget has increased even faster than the growth of population. Though the Cambridgeshire MPs are all Conservatives, the county council itself is a hung council: of the 77 councillors, 30 are Conservative, 25 Alliance, 21 Labour and 1 Independent.

Community development: a style of working

While no council committee or unit is specifically responsible for community development in the county, both officers and councillors are committed to a style of working which includes a community development approach. This is incorporated in the council's document, *Medium Term Planning 1988–1991: Guidelines*. These guidelines, which contain directives on finance and operations, are to be used by every committee in framing policy and practice. The document introduces the concept of the county council's 'brokerage' role. It states:

In addition to its role as a direct provider of services, the council will develop its brokerage role in the effective co-ordination and planning of related services and assets, including those provided by the voluntary and private sectors, and by other public sector agencies. Voluntary services should be encouraged as supplementary to, rather than as a replacement for, statutory services.

Officers saw this reference to outside agencies as indicating the council's commitment to voluntary initiatives and as implicitly recognising community development, though the concept of 'brokerage' remains ambiguous.

Specifically, the guidelines indicate the priority groups and the issues which require inter-departmental co-operation. The groups are frail elderly people, young children and their families, disabled and unemployed people; the issues are the protection of the environment, the prevention of crime, rural communities and the provision of access to countryside. Several of these questions had been considered by working groups which invited community and voluntary representatives to comment. In one particularly impressive working party on crime prevention, the police had worked with several district councils on safe neighbourhood projects. In general, officers approve this style of working on the grounds that it makes planning more sensitive to local needs and, as one of them put it, 'we are more aware of things outside the walls of County Hall'.

Community education

It is the county's community education service which has taken the lead in community development by putting resources into communities and by actively encouraging and stimulating local groups. Cambridgeshire, indeed, is the birthplace of community education, which was pioneered by Henry Morris, the then chief education officer, in 1924. He envisaged the county being served by a network of 'village colleges', each aiming to provide 'a grouping and co-ordination of all the educational and social agencies which now exist in isolation in the countryside'. The county has built on this model and in many areas community education is provided entirely through community schools, the descendants of Henry Morris's village colleges. In some areas, further education colleges have sole or shared responsibility for adult education.

Community schools open their facilities freely to people in their neighbourhoods; and sometimes other facilities are located in them. Three of the community primary schools in Cambridge City, for example, are purpose-built for community use and there is a community tutor in each community secondary school. The schools, adult education centres and youth clubs employ sessional youth workers where necessary and commission halls for classes. In all, there are 47 community education tutors and nine development officers; 45 secondary schools, 30 of which have a community function, and 278 nursery and primary schools, 21 of which have been designated, and nine purpose-built, for community use. The county's community education budget is around £2.5 million.

Community development, as originally defined for our survey, clearly has a major role in the education service. A major review which has recently been carried out proposed to reorganise the community education service and this is now under way. The new structure reflects not only a greater commitment to neighbourhood provision but spells out an explicit function for community development. The policy involves decentralising the co-ordination and planning of the service to three areas – Cambridge, East and South Cambridgeshire; Huntingdon; and Peterborough and Fenland – within which community education resources will be grouped into 'patches', either groupings of schools and centres or schools or centres on their own, according to what is most appropriate for the neighbourhood concerned.

The allocation of resources to the areas is to be calculated according to their population and an assessment of their needs, with four-fifths of the budget going to the patches within an area and one-fifth going to the area as a whole. To monitor needs, a bi-annual planning cycle is envisaged, in which patches will report on their experiences, after liaising with community groups in their area so as to be able to assess their needs more accurately. It is assumed that the areas, being in closer contact with local organisations, such as community associations, will be able to supplement their work more appropriately, for example by funding voluntary organisations, by working with ethnic minorities and by taking account of the special problems of urban and rural deprivation. The area plans and the patch systems are likely to raise the users' expectations, so that the success of the enterprise will depend on the officers' having a sensitive understanding of local issues. In the event, political compromises will have to be made, since community development cannot please all the people all the time. Guidelines are also given for community education staff.

Community development is explicitly defined as being 'concerned with helping people to gain greater control over their lives by increasing their capacity to help themselves and others through community involvement'. Community education in Cambridgeshire brings together two different approaches to educational development, since it supports both the role of the educator, who concentrates on the growth of the individual, and that of the 'social improver', who aims to effect change within the wider community. Community development depended on encouraging citizens to be confident and articulate, some of whom may become 'community leaders'. Traditional community education, which gave mature people a second opportunity of getting an education and enhanced their confidence and skills, had this as its goal. In this sense, community education is following the Workers' Educational Association tradition of self-improvement.

All community education staff are expected to be involved in community development and to give more emphasis to outreach work and to liaising with the community. The problem that they may face in their community development role is recognised in the following safeguarding paragraph:

In emphasising the role of some staff as facilitators of community activity, the service recognises that they may sometimes become involved in helping community groups who are opposed to proposals or actions of public agencies, even the county council itself. The authority accepts that this can be a legitimate role, and accepts the need to support such staff in this potentially contentious area of work.

As this policy is just beginning to be implemented, it will probably take at least two years to see it properly functioning, particularly the patch arrangement. How will these new arrangements, and particularly the community development aspects, be assessed? Since the patches will be required to hold regular meetings with voluntary groups, their work would, in effect, be evaluated by the consumers. However, to avoid evaluations being based only on the opinions of those who use the service, efforts will be made to seek the opinions of the population in general. For example, if a patch had a large ethnic minority, such as the Bengali community in Cambridge City, it would be expected that services would be provided specifically for that community. The service is also to have four inspectors to monitor its work.

Though many community tutors welcomed the reorganisation, and the fact that patches, or neighbourhoods, were being officially recognised, some anxiety was expressed that the schools might come to dominate how the patches were established. In particular, with financial management in their hands, school heads and governors would have control over budgets and might prefer to spend more on conventional school activities rather than community initiatives. Many schools still have a narrow view of the community as comprising only those people who attend it and they have done little to extend their activities to other neighbourhood groups.

Having community development explicitly defined and included in the job descriptions, however, was a positive move. So, too, was the recognition that tutors, and the groups with whom they worked, might sometimes find themselves opposing the county's policies. However, it was likely to be difficult to strike a generally acceptable balance between outreach work and work in the classroom. No policy could lay down set rules; indeed, one tutor said the mix of functions was probably the best way of approaching community development. 'As a tutor I can use the "soft-sell" method; groups emerge slowly. I'd hate to be a dedicated community worker trying to drum up support for this cause or that.'

The Social Services Department

At present, the Social Services involvement in community development entails funding a number of voluntary organisations, especially those which help their major client groups like the elderly, the disabled, and the under fives. The five divisional offices have voluntary services co-ordinators, who recruit and deploy volunteers and are responsible for working with community groups. However, the Social Services Department has now adopted a decentralised, community social work approach, which encourages social workers to be more aware of neighbourhood resources. It also enables clients to get access to those resources more easily, helps to encourage home care and links residential homes more effectively with the local community.

Under this decentralised system, Cambridgeshire is now divided into 19 area teams, dealing with populations of between
10,000 and 40,000, each team being responsible for all social
services provision, fieldwork, community and residential care
within its area. The areas have been defined according to an
analysis of needs and resources which has taken account of client
referral rates, district council and health authority boundaries,
and the boundaries of the communities themselves. The area
teams employ voluntary services co-ordinators who are expected
to liaise with community education staff, district community
development officers, particularly in Peterborough and Cambridge City, and local voluntary groups. While grants to voluntary groups are still made by the county council, area panels, on
which representatives of voluntary organisations in the area sit
alongside local councillors, make the recommendations on
which the allocations are made.

Community education and social services

Whereas the Education Department's approach to the community is to encourage groups as an end in itself, the Social Services
Department regards encouraging community initiatives as a
means to an end. Most community activists considered that
social workers only involved themselves with community groups
when such groups could help meet their clients' needs. Social
services officers confirmed that this was broadly their approach;
services to their clients had to be their first priority, leaving it to
other agencies to do community development. Even though the
proposed pattern of decentralised community social work would
involve social workers more actively in encouraging neighbourhood initiatives, which the voluntary service co-ordinators
would help them to do, given the limitation upon resources, the
department's statutory responsibilities had to be given priority.
Finally, it was interesting to note that, although the Education
Department's proposal for a patch system and the social services
plan for decentralisation were both very detailed documents,
scant reference was made in either to the other department's
proposals.

Cambridgeshire Community Council

One of the most readable documents on community life in the
county is *Cambridgeshire Villages, a Guide to Local Facilities*. Produced by Cambridgeshire Community Council, the *Guide* lists

the facilities in the 316 Cambridgeshire villages, ranging from food shops to banks, doctors' surgeries to halls, schools to teashops. The *Guide* also monitors the rate at which village amenities are being lost and gives examples of how to lobby for resources and organise self-help projects. The growth of self-help initiatives in the county has been so great that the *Guide* has listed these under the following headings: transport, social care schemes, community shops, bulk buying, play-groups, over-sixties clubs, disabled groups, education groups, support to the voluntary sector and other initiatives. An excellent hand-book for community development, the *Guide* sums up the community council's role as being to monitor trends in the county, to encourage the public discussion of issues, to support voluntary bodies throughout the county, to help set up new voluntary organisations and to promote community development projects.

The community council has a team of four development officers, as well as a parish councils officer and a rural officer. The work is overseen by a director, with an Executive Committee made up of councillors from the county and district councils and representatives of local councils for voluntary service. With an annual expenditure of around £100,000, the council is mainly funded by the Development Commission (£38,000) and by the county council (£11,000), which also gives it £22,000 specifically for the development officers.

Among its many activities, the council organises care groups, sets up volunteer bureaux, produces research reports and organises play schemes. Its director summed up its role as that of 'speaking out' and working where other agencies could not operate. As the council was independent of the statutory authorities, communities trusted it to express their views. This independence was especially important for the four development workers, whose work in the villages often led them to challenge the activities of the county council, a role which the county accepted. As one senior county council officer said, 'if we employed rural development officers, I think villages would be a little suspicious. It's more effective if their role is carried out by the Community Council'. The development officers worked alongside the county's community education tutors, and the community council thought it sensible for the community education service to accept the boundaries of existing neighbourhoods and communities as their local areas. The community council also approved of the Social Services promoting care groups throughout the county and the fact that the voluntary sector was involved, through the Joint Development Teams, with the Social Services and the region's district health authorities.

Community Development in Cambridgeshire

Cambridgeshire County Council, as a strategic planning authority, is very sensitive to community issues and its officers are well-informed about the needs of communities within Cambridgeshire. This sensitivity, however, is not matched with a standing committee or a specialist unit, for example, which could ensure that community development was taken seriously in the allocation of resources. The county council did not consider it would be viable to set up a special community development unit, given the large number of departments that it would have to oversee. It was far more economical to ensure that the separate departments and committees were fully aware of local needs so that they could each take their own community development initiatives, working together with other departments where necessary. It was thought that, while rural development could be carried out by a special unit, this was best done by the community council which was independent of the local authority. Indeed, the community council thought that increased discussion of, and even opposition to the county council policies, was a measure of its success in promoting community development. As for community development in the urban areas, the county looked to Cambridge City and Peterborough, with their structures for community services and strong councils for voluntary service, to deal with them.

6 Thamesdown: From Paternalism to Participation

Thamesdown came into being with the reorganisation of local government in 1974, which brought the former borough of Swindon and the adjacent rural areas into one new local authority. Swindon, which houses 85 per cent of the district's population of 163,000, is the core of the district. In their analysis of types of towns, Donnison and Soto defined Swindon as part of 'middle England', an area that contained somewhat nondescript towns which had no university, no buildings of any special architectural merit and which were rarely featured in the press; towns which people might have heard of but did not know much about. 'These are not the places in which groups dominating Britain and its "establishment" spend much time and give much thought to,' they wrote.

Since the early nineteenth century, when Swindon was a rather poor market town serving a local agrarian economy, it has changed dramatically. In 1841, the Great Western Railway (GWR) established its engineering works there, which soon became the dominant place of employment in the town. With its growth, Swindon was transformed from a small, stagnating market town into a thriving industrial centre, which stood in sharp contrast, economically, politically and socially, to the predominantly rural county of Wiltshire within which it was set. By the early part of this century, the boom had ended and the railway industry in Swindon had begun to decline. But the economic uncertainty of the inter-war period began to change with the outbreak of the Second World War, when firms like Vickers and Plessey opened factories to support the war effort. These factories remained and developed in the post-war period, opening up new employment opportunities for the borough's growing population.

This chapter has been written by Maurice Broady.

The subsequent development of the town was given a considerable impetus when Swindon became an expanding town under the Town Development Act 1952. Expanding towns complemented the new towns and shared the same objectives, being intended to receive overspill population and industry from the major conurbations, in Swindon's case from London. Under the guidance and on the initiative of an enterprising and ambitious town clerk, Swindon seized this excellent opportunity to grow.

The town expanded rapidly. Large estates were built to house the thousands of new arrivals and new industry was attracted to the town to provide jobs. Prosperity increased, wages improved and the proportion of owner-occupiers and car owners rose substantially. As the population grew, so did the town's social and cultural facilities; and though the kind of industrial and commercial development has changed, this expansion has continued into the 1980s. Swindon now lies within the 'sunrise corridor' along the M4 motorway, which stretches from London to Bristol.

Swindon's social development

Throughout these various phases of economic expansion, Thamesdown Borough Council, like its predecessor, has been keen to ensure that relevant social objectives were also met and that newcomers settled in quickly and had access to community facilities. This has been one of the main reasons for the interest which the council has shown in community development.

But this concern for what we now call community development can be traced back to the dominance and paternalistic traditions of the GWR, which provided housing and other social facilities to keep its workforce healthy and content. As the railway industry declined, however, the local council began to take a number of social initiatives which clearly expressed a paternalistic notion of intervention. The council had tried to set up community centres during the Second World War, largely without success. But the impetus for a broader community development policy emerged with the town expansion programmes of the 1950s since the borough council was keen to ensure that the newcomers settled in happily and mixed easily with the existing residents.

In the early stages of this town expansion, the council adopted two main policies for social development. First, they provided common rooms on each new estate and, second, they employed neighbourhood workers, who were usually qualified social workers, to work on these estates. These workers were originally responsible to the town clerk; but when the post of social development officer was established, it was he who took charge of these initiatives. The approach was later described as providing 'somewhere to go' and 'someone to turn to for help'. The common rooms were small multi-purpose halls with ancillary rooms that could be hired from the council by any of the community groups on the estate.

The provision of neighbourhood workers was particularly innovative at the time. As they were not attached to any particular agency and had no administrative or financial responsibilities, they were able to develop their work with the greatest of freedom. Living on the new estates in which they worked, their main task was to establish a stable and functioning community, from which they could eventually withdraw. In this way, they tried to avoid creating any sense of dependency, aiming on the contrary to help these communities to stand firmly on their own feet. An important element in their work was to welcome all newcomers on to the estates and help them settle down. They also monitored the social progress of the estates and reported to the social development officer what was happening and if there was any need for policy changes. All this was standard, traditional community development work.

Michael Harloe, in his review of this policy, concludes that these early initiatives were mostly successful and that the neighbourhood workers did a lot of useful work in stimulating community development on the estates. Nevertheless, this policy focused far too narrowly on problems of social life and leisure and failed to deal with the many wider issues such as unemployment which, despite its expansion, was still a major problem affecting the town. This is a criticism which to some extent is still valid today. Furthermore, the paternalism of the GWR days continued to affect the borough council, which retained full control of social development policy and seemed reluctant to give the residents any opportunity to control the facilities which had been provided, still less to have any influence on policy questions.

By the early 1960s, these drawbacks had become increasingly apparent as the communities in Swindon began to grow and develop. They soon began to outgrow the rather limited service that was being offered them and the social development work began to decline. In 1968, however, that social development policy was rescued from obscurity, as its emphasis changed so that community development began to be seen in relation to the whole town and not just to the new estates. Efforts also began to be made to encourage a much closer working relationship with local communities and to break away from the earlier paternalistic approach. This was the seed-bed of the current community development initiatives which will be considered in the following sections.

The organisation of community development

Compared with most other local authorities, Thamesdown's approach to community development is very distinctive. First, there is a special committee, the Community Planning Committee, which has full responsibility for this area of work. Second, there is a separate department of 27 officers called the Community Development Division. The existence of this committee and department indicates the degree to which the borough council is committed to community development.

The Community Development Division (CDD) was established in the early 1970s as part of the council's Development and Corporate Planning Group. Following the reorganisation of local government in 1974, it became part of the Development and Housing Group, until it was decided to form a completely separate Housing Department. Community development was then transferred to the Chief Executive's Department. At this stage, an attempt was made to locate community development within the Arts and Recreation Group, a move which, had it succeeded, would have seriously reduced its significance and put the Community Planning Committee on a par with, say, the Leisure Gardens Sub-Committee. Eventually, after an internal reorganisation in the summer of 1986, the community development department was placed within the newly-formed Economic and Social Development Group.

The CDD is now one of four divisions within this group, along with Employment Development, Development and Project Management and Property Management and Valuation. The division is therefore located within a group that is concerned with the development of the town as a whole rather than with the more restricted function of leisure, which would have been the case if it had been put into the Arts and Recreation Group.

Since its inception in 1974, the borough council has

wholeheartedly endorsed community development. Its policy is to encourage a flexible approach that avoids a bureaucratic style and can readily adapt to change. Its aims have been restated recently as '. . . developing conditions for a full social, cultural, working and recreational life for the people of the area, comprising a participating, just and caring community'. Indeed, the importance attached to this field of work is also indicated in the objectives of the Community Planning Committee:

. . . ensuring as far as possible a fully human quality of community life, with special emphasis on the removal of social deprivation and the encouragement of opportunities for people to develop to their full potential, including, of course, their social responsibility and interdependence.

The Community Planning Committee, which is the focal point for all community development undertaken by the borough and one of its most important committees, was also formed in 1974, following local government reorganisation. Members are keen to sit on it as it is a very active and politically important committee. At present, it has 18 members: 13 Labour, 3 Conservative and 2 SDP/Alliance. Though this is clearly a Labour-dominated committee within an overwhelmingly Labour council, the contributions which are made by members of the other parties reflect their equal commitment to community development. The members of the Community Planning Committee are very keen to get out into the community as much as possible to meet with local residents and to discuss their problems.

The main committee has a number of sub-committees, including the General Purposes, the Race Relations and the Community Centres Sub-Committees. The participation of lay members in this committee structure is positively encouraged, a lay member having recently been elected chairman of the Race Relations Sub-Committee. This was the first sub-committee actually to encourage lay members to participate, following the recommendations of the Youth in a Multi-Racial Society Working Party in 1982. The Community Centres Sub-Committee, which was established in 1986 following a Working Party on Community Centre Design, in order to oversee community centre policy, also includes lay representatives who are elected through the Local Federation of Community Organisations.

A number of working parties have also been set up to consider particular issues; they report to the Community Planning and other relevant committees. As well as the Youth in a Multi-Racial Society Working Party, there is a Social Strategy Working Party, reporting to the Policy and Resources Committee, which is trying to develop a strategy for tackling poverty and deprivation; a Women's Issues Working Party which is dealing with the needs of women in Thamesdown and a working party under the Race Relations Sub-Committee that is studying the question of Section 11 posts within the authority. A Working Party on Unemployment, which was also initiated by the social development officer, subsequently became the Local Employment Initiatives Sub-Committee of the Policy and Resources Committee and is now regarded as a very important sub-committee indeed. The setting up of working parties is therefore standard practice in Thamesdown, which can often lead to a full sub-committee on that subject being established.

The head of the Community Development Division is the social development officer. He or she is responsible for managing the division, for advising the council on social policy and for the development work on a number of projects. The division consists of an administrative section, the fieldwork teams and the Social Policy Unit.

The administrative section has five staff who are responsible for administering the division, for managing the eleven social halls located on the various estates and for handling the borough's grants to voluntary organisations and for a number of charities, such as the Mayor's Helping Hand Fund, which the borough runs. The Social Policy Unit, with three staff, was set up in 1985 because fieldworkers were becoming increasingly involved in town-wide issues which they had neither the time nor resources to handle. The unit's function is to undertake inquiries into relevant problems, which have recently included women's issues and the borough council's role in health care.

By far the largest section within the division are the fieldwork teams which have increased steadily in recent years and now have 21 members. The town is covered by four area teams, each led by a community development officer, with a staff of neighbourhood workers and other specialists whose job descriptions are very broad. There is also a Community Centres Team which is responsible for managing the community centres and social halls in the borough and for liaising with the various community groups which manage these buildings.

In addition to this, two members of the community development staff work in the Ike Gradwell Community Suite in the recently developed Link Centre Complex. This is an interesting example of collaboration between the division and Arts and Recreation, which is responsible for running most of the Links Centre Complex, though getting staff from these two departments to work together is not without its problems, since each has a different philosophy of community development. Staff from the division are not deployed in rural areas of the borough, but the senior community development officer may respond to any initiatives which develop in these areas. The Social Services Department of the county council also employs community development officers who cover the rural areas. Their role is somewhat different to the fieldwork staff employed by Thamesdown, however, since they are appointed to support specific client groups, like luncheon clubs and day centres, and do not have a general developmental role.

The value that the borough places on neighbourhood work is indicated by the fact that neighbourhood workers are encouraged to live in the areas they are working in so as to maximise their contact with their communities; and most neighbourhood workers currently employed do in fact live in their own patches. This is a vital aspect of their approach to community development. Fieldworkers are also encouraged to produce detailed community profiles for the Community Planning Committee, collating physical, social and economic data on their areas which can be of great value to workers, councillors and residents. They also help new workers to get to know their patches and to make out cases for additional staff resources.

The Community Development Division clearly recognises the importance of being as flexible as possible in its work in order to be able to respond to issues as they crop up. But as it has grown in recent years, it has been necessary to introduce a more complex administrative structure in order to co-ordinate and control its workload. Within the last two or three years, the division has begun to set priorities for action. The two major objectives are to tackle poverty and deprivation and to encourage the community to participate fully in the affairs of the council. These priorities are very broad so as not to restrict workers unnecessarily in taking up issues or initiatives, but it is expected that all their work should contribute to one or both of these objectives.

Finally, as the division has grown, it has become necessary to hold quarterly division meetings, as well as the monthly team meetings, where all the staff can meet to share information and exchange ideas. These meetings go on all day and are usually held outside the office, away from telephones and other interruptions. In the morning each team reports on its activities, while the afternoon session is given over to discussing a specific issue that bears on the work of the Division.

The wider context
Like many other municipal departments, the Community Development Division is relatively self-contained and it tends to be viewed rather suspiciously by other departments which do not really understand the nature and purpose of community development. The Community Development Division accordingly is often mistakenly regarded as a bunch of left-wing activists, stirring up communities and thereby creating problems and unnecessary work for other departments of the borough. Indeed, this impression is strengthened by the fact that the only contact that some departments have with the division is over particular problems or contentious issues, so that it is perceived rather

negatively as a source of trouble. However, relationships have improved over the years and other departments are slowly becoming more sympathetic, especially as the division often advises them if they are consulting with the public. Even so, there appears to be little formal liaison with the Arts and Recreation Department, which is the only other department to have any community development staff, though they seem to have good working relationships on specific projects.

With Wiltshire County Council, the degree of liaison varies. Since Thamesdown includes the largest urban area in Wiltshire, where the needs are greatest, it absorbs a large amount of the county council's resources and county councillors in the more rural and affluent parts of the county find it difficult to understand the problems that exist in the inner areas of Swindon. The county council employs community development workers in the Social Services Department and the Youth and Community Service. Thamesdown certainly works closely with the Social Services Department, with whose local officers it appears to have a very good relationship. The relationships with the Youth and Community Service, though they could be better, are steadily improving. In fact, the division has recently held a joint team meeting with local Youth and Community staff to discuss matters of mutual interest, which it is hoped will lead to closer links being fostered between the two departments.

The links which the division sustains with the community are understandably strong. Swindon in particular is vibrant with large numbers of community groups and voluntary organisations. In addition, there is a strong network of community councils which Thamesdown has encouraged, of which residents are automatically members. These councils are elected annually and have the potential to contribute to the division's policy making. In reality, however, since many community councils are also responsible for running community centres, which in most cases takes up most of their time, they do not make that kind of contribution.

A Community Forum was also set up a number of years ago to try to make this possible. The division acts as the secretariat of the forum, but it has not met recently. The forum initially identifies issues and then calls meetings of all interested community groups, voluntary organisations, officers and members to discuss them. These meetings have sometimes influenced the borough council. For example, if the Arts and Recreation Department has plans to provide a new play area, it will now automatically call a public meeting. The influence of the Community Forum has also ensured that all community councils now receive the agendas of the Planning and Community Planning Committees at the same time as the members, so that they can make their views known in good time for the relevant meetings. The encouragement which lay members are given to participate in committees is another avenue through which the community has the opportunity to influence policy.

Both officers and members seem willing to encourage the wider community to participate in borough policy making. Community development, which is a vital aspect of borough policy, is certainly very high on the political agenda. This can be judged by the fact that, although the borough has been rate-capped for the last three years, the community development budget has continued to grow, despite the fact that the division is not an income-generating department, while other departments have suffered cuts. Staff numbers have also increased each year, with one new neighbourhood worker being appointed in 1987/88. However, though it is doubtful whether staff numbers will continue to increase, this in no way reflects any lack of support from the borough council.

There is clearly a close working relationship between officers and members, and members spoke very highly of the work and the enthusiasm of the division's officers. Sometimes, however, officers had to be very sensitive to their relationship with councillors as some of them still felt somewhat threatened by the role of the fieldwork staff, whom they thought were in effect doing their job. Indeed, community development work can often raise difficulties for the local government officers concerned, since they may be involved in campaigns that bring them into direct conflict with their employers. This problem is not very common within the division, but, if it should ever become an issue, then it was felt that the officer concerned would be backed both by members and the senior officers.

This close working relationship between officers and members arises first, from their common commitment to community development and, second, from the small size of the town and the fact that members and officers meet frequently outside their normal, formal relationships. Finally, a very clear distinction appears to be made between the 'professional' and the 'political' aspects of community development work, the officers being the professionals who use their skills to identify local need and the members the politicians who translate those needs into policy.

Community development practice

The three features that characterise Thamesdown's community development work are: that it is strongly supported by paid staff; that community centres and social halls are extensively provided; and that relatively large sums are given in grant aid to voluntary organisations and community groups.

The fact that Thamesdown has a full-time community development staff in a clearly identifiable division confirms the borough's commitment to this work and helps local people to appreciate this fact. Representatives of the voluntary sector commented that the fact that staff were available to help them was one of the most valuable aspects of Thamesdown's policy, since it indicated the importance which the borough assigned to neighbourhood development and helped neighbourhoods become aware of what they might achieve. It also gives the work much greater standing and public credibility than it would otherwise have and this makes it easier for the division to influence other departments within the authority. Furthermore, the setting up of the Social Policy Unit has enabled the division to respond more effectively to issues, such as health and women, to monitor progress and to act as a central liaison point for other departments and agencies. It is also in a good position to provide an overview of policy issues which fieldworkers have often found it difficult to manage, working as they do under considerable pressure in specific localities.

The provision of community buildings has also been an important element in Thamesdown's approach. As Swindon grew in the 1950s, the council provided not only neighbourhood workers to help newcomers settle in to their new environment but social halls or tenants' common rooms to serve as social centres on each estate, where people could meet each other and help in developing their own community. Today, Thamesdown's policy is to provide a community centre in every housing area in the town. There are currently 24 such centres and there would be more if the resources were available. Whereas social halls are owned by the borough and hired out to community groups, community centres are built by the council but are then handed over to the community associations to manage. The use of these two kinds of community building has by and large been successful.

The borough covers the cost of maintaining the external fabric of the community centres and charges the associations a pepper-corn rent, while the associations themselves remain responsible for their internal maintenance and running costs. The council, however, does provide grants to help them meet these costs – in 1986/87, nearly £53,000 – in addition to the general grants referred to later on. Since the council recognises that it is not easy for volunteers to run buildings, a Community Centres Team has been established to offer support, advice and training to community associations. A Community Centres Sub-Committee has also been set up on the recommendation of the Community Centres Working Party.

These community associations also raise their own funds to cover the costs of running their buildings. The licensed bars, which are also run in many community centres, cause problems. First, they often generate a high cash turnover which creates difficulties in administering the centres and managing their fi-nances. Second, the bars tend to make the centres more like working men's clubs and sometimes fail to meet the needs of the community as a whole since the bar begins to dominate the life of the centre so that the other activities suffer. To allay these anxieties, the borough does not allow a bar to be opened until a new community centre has been open for at least a year or until the officers and members are satisfied that it can be run for the benefit of the whole community; nor may the bar occupy more than 10 per cent of the total area of the centre. As the commun-ity centres are relatively self-contained, the community develop-ment fieldwork staff avoid using them as bases in order to prevent themselves becoming too centre-oriented.

Although the borough provides community centres, some-times the local residents have actively campaigned for one. In the Pinehurst area of Swindon, local people, helped by the borough, have fought a long battle to convert an old school building into the Pinehurst People's Centre. The money to finance the project came from a complex land deal which in-volved lands declared surplus by Wiltshire County Council. The division is currently very concerned by the fact that the county has disposed of a number of school playing fields within Thamesdown which the borough could have made good use of, but which they now have to compete for in the open market at greatly inflated values. In Pinehurst, the community council encouraged all the local groups to support a project to ensure its survival for the benefit of the whole community. The building will ultimately provide space for a number of activities including a play-group, a housing advice office, the Thamesdown Community Arts Project, the Unemployed Woodwork Group and community industry.

The third major element in Thamesdown's community development policy is its programme of grant aid for community groups and voluntary organisations. The Community Planning Committee is the major funding committee but the Policy and Resources Committee also provides grants for employment initiatives and the Arts and Recreation Committee for sporting activities. Grants are also made by the county council's Social Services and Education Committees. Within Thamesdown, the Community Development Division acts as the clearing house for grant applications, deciding which authority is the most appropriate one to approach in each case. The Administrative Section of the division helps groups to make these applications, but shortage of staff has limited its ability to assist groups as much as it would like.

Thamesdown has been funding groups for over twenty years since the early town expansion began and the level of funding has grown substantially, particularly within the last five years. In the early 1980s, the council was funding about twenty groups but in 1987/88 well over fifty groups have received grants ranging from £200 to £50,000. The budget has increased every year until 1988/89 when it is over £300,000, but it is doubtful if it will be possible to increase this sum in the future.

These grants are awarded annually. Thamesdown does not have strict rules or any statement of criteria for allocating grants, and it appears to fund schemes on their individual merits. The decisions are made by the borough council upon recommendations from a grants panel, which is made up of members and officers from the borough, the county council and the health authority. Until last year, each group applying for funding has had to put its case in person to the panel but this proved to be extremely time-consuming, so this year it has been decided that the grants panel will only interview new groups and those applying for large increases. However, as the borough still wishes to keep in contact with the groups it currently funds, it is arranging a series of special evenings at which groups working in similar fields can discuss their work and exchange their views and experiences. Grant funding helps to support a wide range of

groups and organisations which make an invaluable contribution
to the well-being of the local community.

Thamesdown is very fortunate in being able to call on other
important sources of grant aid, including the Allied Dunbar
Charitable Trust and the Thamesdown Community Trust.
Allied Dunbar grew out of Hambro Life Assurance, which set up
its headquarters in Swindon in 1971. They allocate a percentage
of their profits to the charitable trust (approximately £100,000
per annum), from which they fund voluntary organisations, most
of them in Swindon. They employ two workers to liaise with
community groups and deal with the grants. The Thamesdown
Community Trust was set up in 1975 and obtains its funds from
local firms.

The effectiveness of Thamesdown's community development policy

It is very difficult to judge precisely whether community development initiatives have been successful since success is difficult to
quantify and the quality of provision is not always easy to assess.
The Community Development Division is at present trying to
evaluate the effectiveness of its work by finding out whether
resources are actually reaching those who are most in need; but
this is also proving very difficult to do. Certainly, Thamesdown
does encourage a wide range of community development initiatives and, compared with many other local authorities, the
borough's community development work is very advanced. Nor
is there any question that community development has had a
significant effect on the town, as can be seen in the considerable
public support which it receives, the commitment which it
inspires among both the officers and the members of the borough
council, the comprehensive grant funding and in the vibrancy of
the voluntary sector and the large numbers of community groups
that exist.

How far community groups can influence the borough's community development policy is, however, questionable. For
though Swindon is alive with community groups and voluntary
organisations, with which in general Thamesdown's relationship
is good, the administration of the community development policy within the borough is highly centralised. Since the borough
council is so dominant in this field, all community development
work is channelled through the authority. Community groups
may be using community centres provided by the borough, work-

ing with borough staff or be actually funded by the Community Planning Committee. The control of policy rests with that committee and the division and such opportunities as are available for the community itself to influence their policies are not well used. The Community Forum, for example, has not met for two years. A cynical observer might therefore be inclined to argue that Thamesdown's approach is still influenced by the paternalism which it inherited from the GWR days.

The comprehensive grant system, commendable as it is, is not without its problems. As is so often the case, the fact that grants are awarded annually makes long-term planning rather difficult for the voluntary sector, so that even those groups which are funded still feel insecure. It would be preferable, of course, to fund groups for up to three years, as part of a rolling programme subject to annual review, since this would make it easier for them to work towards long-term objectives. But given the resource constraints under which Thamesdown is increasingly having to operate and central government's continuing interference in local government spending, it might be difficult for the council to guarantee grants for a three-year period. Nevertheless, the Community Planning Committee has recently recommended to the Policy and Resources Committee that grants to voluntary bodies should be given on a three-year basis.

The elaborate process whereby groups have had to present their case to a panel of officers and members also gives the impression that they must approach the local authority cap in hand. This may also appear to be somewhat paternalistic, the more so since the groups always seem grateful to receive what they get, even if it is much less than they have asked for. The one year funding policy may also indicate the council's unwillingness to surrender power and control. However, the system is being changed to make it less intimidating for voluntary groups and less time-consuming for the officers and members involved.

The other major problem affecting grant aid in Swindon is that most of the money for grants is obtained, as in many local authorities, under section 137 of the Local Government Act 1972. This allows local authorities to raise funds up to the product of a two penny rate, which can be used to cover expenditure which, in the local authority's opinion, is in the interests of all or part of its area or of its inhabitants. The Community Planning Committee has always received the lion's share of the funds which are raised in this way, but because the claims on resources have increased so much in recent years, Thamesdown is very close to its maximum limit so that further growth is considered unlikely.

A further problem is the fact that Thamesdown no longer qualifies for Urban Aid. As a result, a number of time-expired projects, including the Afro-Caribbean Centre and the Thamesdown Law Centre, have had to be funded by the council. Under the Urban Aid scheme, 75 per cent of the costs were funded by the Department of the Environment, with the local authorities finding the remaining 25 per cent. In the case of the Thamesdown Law Centre, in 1987/88 the county contributed 17.5 per cent and the borough 7.5 per cent of this sum, and this has resulted in an additional claim being made on increasingly scarce resources. As Thamesdown wants these and other affected projects to continue, additional funds will have to be found.

The future of Thamesdown's community development policy is therefore going to be influenced by the degree to which it can get more resources. The Community Development Division, having enjoyed much political and financial support over the years, has been able to expand considerably in recent years. But its future growth is now uncertain. Thamesdown has not only suffered from the recent alterations to the Urban Programme but it has also been rate-capped for the fourth year in succession. While it will clearly continue to give community development its whole-hearted support, the council's ability to transform that support into positive action will probably be increasingly restricted.

The borough's community development policy has undoubtedly improved its relationship with, and its responsiveness to the community. As a result of pressure and support from the Community Development Division, local authority officers from other departments are now more willing, and better able to deal directly with community groups. Furthermore, the borough's policies have had a significant effect in supporting the strong and vital voluntary sector within Thamesdown, which makes an invaluable contribution to the well-being of the community.

A unique partnership has in fact developed between Thamesdown and the voluntary sector. This is particularly well illustrated by their joint agreement over rate-capping. The voluntary sector agreed to support the council's stand on rate-capping, which in turn pledged that there would be no redundancies or cuts in its support for voluntary organisations. Voluntary sector workers are also encouraged to join the same union as the local government officers which adds strength and cohesion to their relationship. Consequently, the voluntary sector has to a large extent been protected from the full ravages of rate-capping.

Thamesdown's community development policy clearly follows a pluralist model, with a strong belief in the value of social democracy and in the principles of consultation and participation. Community development is therefore seen in quite a traditional way with a focus upon encouraging and supporting community activities within the neighbourhoods and an emphasis on helping groups articulate their needs to which the authority can respond. The Community Development Division is recognised to be the means by which the authority becomes more responsive to community needs. It is often seen as a buffer between the community and the local authority which, like a sponge, soaks up all the aggravation from within the community and then feeds the community's ideas into the system. There also appears to be a clear distinction between community development work which is done by the officers and the political issues which remain the responsibility of the councillors.

It is open to question whether issues such as unemployment, poverty and inequality can ever be successfully tackled by this approach. These problems extend well beyond the boundaries of one local authority and they can only be effectively dealt with by a far more comprehensive and co-ordinated policy than is likely to be adopted successfully within the current structure of local government. With this limitation recognised, Thamesdown's community development policies have certainly improved the quality of life for its residents. They provide both the opportunity and the resources for groups and individuals to take up issues which can benefit the whole community. The factors that have made this possible are the comprehensive nature of its community development policies, the degree of commitment among its officers and members, the fact that ambitious projects are tackled in a positive and innovative way and, above all, the borough's genuine concern to encourage community participation.

7 Newcastle upon Tyne: Different Approaches

Newcastle's pride strikes visitors as soon as they get off the train. The splendid sweep of its early Victorian station and its fine stone buildings bespeak the city's rapid development in the nineteenth century. A major bridge-town on the River Tyne, Newcastle's prosperity was founded upon its shipbuilding, engineering and commerce. But in the period between the wars, as once again in recent years, Tyneside suffered acutely from economic depression. Thus, while the city's status as a regional, commercial and administrative capital is embodied in the handsome new buildings that stand alongside the old in the city centre, this appearance of prosperity belies the serious deprivation which afflicts many other parts of the city.

In 1981, of the 36 metropolitan districts in England, Newcastle upon Tyne was in the top quartile for male unemployment (18.4 per cent) and for council tenancies (45.7 per cent); it had the second highest proportion of people over retirement age (19.5 per cent), the lowest percentage (20.2 per cent) of young people under the age of 16 and the third highest percentage of single parent families (8.0 per cent). It is mainly as a response to this high level of deprivation that community development has been encouraged in the city in the last fifteen years or so.

In a city which is relatively small in geographical spread, the areas of most acute deprivation mostly lie in the riverside wards that run from Scotswood in the west to Walker in the east. In these wards, the average unemployment rate in 1981 was 27.2 per cent, while in Walker it was 29.7 per cent and in Scotswood as high as 33.6 per cent. These were mostly areas in which the

---

This chapter has been written by Mike Beazley.

population had declined by at least 10 per cent in the period 1971–81, but the figure rose to 20 per cent in most of these wards, and in Byker to 35.5 per cent. This decline had left behind a population in which, in roughly one household in every five, there was one pensioner living alone in areas where, on average, about 7.0 per cent of all households were also over-crowded (against the average for Newcastle of 4.6 per cent). These very crude statistics demonstrate how socially and econo-mically deprived these riverside wards were, and still are.

The city council's role in community development

Community development, as a function of the city council, has been especially concerned with these nine districts along the river which, together with five outer estates which share their high levels of deprivation, now constitute the city's 14 Priority Areas. This interest in community development dates from the late 1960s and, in particular, from 1974, when the city became a metropolitan district, with a Labour council which has held office ever since. It is especially noteworthy, since it has grown in a city with a tradition of strong, efficient and relatively centralised local government. Its administration has been de-scribed as paternalistic, since it long held it to be the city council's sole responsibility to provide public services, including social welfare, and since neither the voluntary sector nor the local community played any significant part in its corporate thinking.

Nevertheless, by the time the new council took office in 1974, a number of community development projects had already been started in the city. Following the Skeffington Committee's report on public participation in planning, the Northumberland and Tyneside Council of Social Service had begun a project in Byker which involved the local people in replanning the area, while the Community Projects Foundation was promoting another in Scotswood which campaigned on housing issues and led to the foundation first of the Scotswood Tenants' Association and, later, of the Scotswood Community Project. Even more signifi-cant for its influence on the subsequent development of com-munity work in the city, in 1973 the council finally agreed to one of the 12 Community Development Projects funded by the Home Office being set up in the Benwell ward, where Jeremy Beacham, soon to become the leader of the council, was one of the councillors.

The city council's changing attitude to the voluntary sector was also signalled by its inviting the voluntary organisations to apply for grant aid in a 'partnership of service' covering the whole range of social need. This invitation laid the foundations for the support of the voluntary sector which the council has continued ever since. The new council quickly established a policy of improving conditions in the most deprived riverside wards, in 1976 setting up its Priority Area Teams, which confirmed the city's commitment to community development, and two years later led to Newcastle's being designated as an Inner City Partnership under the government's Urban Programme.

The effect of these initial steps can be clearly seen in the way the city now conducts its affairs. Thus, the social services budget for 1987/88 included about £850,000 in grant aid for some 60 voluntary organisations and £60,000 for their work with children under the age of five, while other grants and financial support amounted to an additional £4 million. Furthermore, 67 staff are now employed in community development sections in four departments of the council: the Community Services section of the Social Services Department (13); the Priority Areas section of the Chief Executive's Department (11); the Youth and Community section of the Education Department (32); and the Community Recreation section of the Leisure and Recreation Department (11).

The growth of community development work over such a disparate range of municipal departments has been fostered by an alliance between the leaders of the Labour group and a number of sympathetic officers. Recently, however, the question has been raised as to whether it would be more efficient and cost-effective to amalgamate some, or all of these strands of work into one department. Thus the council, seeing little difference between the activities that were promoted in sports centres and youth and community centres, in 1983 set up a Joint Sub-Committee to consider how far their approaches overlapped. Their concern evidently broadened, for in April 1986 it considered a set of papers on *Community Work in Newcastle*, which grew out of the officers' concern at the recent increase 'in the number of Council officers in a number of departments who have been designated "community roles"'. It suggested that a 'greater understanding of community work methods and philosophy may help the ways in which the authority responds to issues raised at a community level'. This account will consider the kind of work that is being done by the four departments of the local authority before returning to these more recent developments.

Priority Area Teams

Priority Area Teams (PATs) have been very influential in promoting the council's community development work, since they have devolved to the neighbourhoods some responsibility for allocating extra resources to meet local needs. The idea derived from the city council's concern to combat 'stress' in the city's priority areas, as part of a wider set of policies which main-line departments were to promote for improving income maintenance and social opportunities. In what is described as a 'modified form of neighbourhood management', the council set up Priority Area Teams comprising the three ward councillors, with field officers from relevant departments in attendance, one of whom co-ordinated their work. They were intended to alert the council to 'local views on major needs and projects affecting their areas' by identifying their particular needs, putting up proposals for meeting them and initiating action upon those proposals.

The teams were to compete for claims upon a budget, initially £110,000, which now stands at £300,000. In making these claims, the local knowledge of social and economic conditions was to be tapped and residents, tenants' and community groups were to be encouraged to play an active part. However, since local groups might well misinterpret the council's intentions and see the fund mistakenly as 'being available to support their own particular special interests', it was made clear that decisions were to be made by the teams of councillors and officers and that formal communications with the council were to remain through the ward councillors. It was expected that the social needs and circumstances in the various wards would vary considerably and PATs were encouraged to be flexible in their approach.

While these teams are now an established part of the city's administration, how they operate differs from the original conception. Based originally in the Planning Department (all bar one of the original PAT leaders were planners), when that department reverted to a more limited role in physical planning, the PATs were in 1981 placed in the Chief Executive's Department. They have promoted projects which have been generally appreciated in the localities and have improved communications between councillors and the representatives of local organisations. Their participation in the work of the PATs has been stimulated mainly by their desire to claim extra resources from the special local budgets which are under the teams' control, while the councillors have benefitted from increased contacts and better communications in their wards and by being able to allocate relatively small sums to local projects.

But the public at large has not participated in these local forums. This is partly because some councillors have not encouraged any wider participation, being sceptical of the contributions which ordinary members of the public might be able to make. Often too, partly because appropriate local meeting places are lacking, team meetings have been held in the Civic Centre, where the relatively formal atmosphere has tended to dissuade local people from attending and from contributing easily to the discussions. Nevertheless, in the first four years, a third of the projects which the PATs carried out were responses to requests from local voluntary organisations like tenants' groups or Age Concern.

Nor has the Priority Areas sub-committee exploited its potential as a forum for discussing inner-city issues interdepartmentally, despite the fact that it is chaired by the leader of the council and brings together representatives of many departments. Indeed, the PATs have been unable directly to influence committee decisions, as it was originally expected that local councillors would do by remitting matters raised in the PATs directly to the main committees. At worst, some remits have been lost in the administrative system. More generally, the teams have been able to provide local people with information about a committee's operations which might not otherwise have been so readily available. But team officers' views have tended to be discounted as being 'generalist' both by departments which have claimed a special professional expertise and by councillors who, having wider interests to consider as members of major committees, have hesitated to fight for their own wards.

The main-line departments have seen the PATs as useful primarily for communicating downwards or as providing more money for what they themselves wished to do in the wards. The Housing Department even thought that the teams had aims that conflicted with its own and would have preferred more resources to have been allocated to the Area Housing Management Committees rather than to specific projects decided upon and funded directly by the teams. Thus, though the teams have helped to make departments aware of new needs, such as the problems of the disabled, they have not had any direct effect upon the committees' decisions, still less influenced directly their spending patterns or policies. Nevertheless, the fact that there is a Priority Areas sub-committee has meant that the council's community development role has been formally recognised, while many developments, like its active support of voluntary groups and its fostering of local recreational facilities, have been helped on by the initiatives and experience of particular PATs.

The Community Services section

The community development role of the PATs has been most closely paralleled by the work of the Social Services Department's Community Services section, which shares their concern with poverty and stress. The department itself has taken a very positive view of community development. Even before the local government structure was changed in 1974, it was responsible for carrying out the council's progressive policy of grant aiding voluntary organisations and had also started community development projects with Urban Aid funding. With the social workers' strike in 1979, the department's managerial structure was reorganised and community projects were no longer managed *ad hoc* by area social work teams. The creation of the post of senior assistant (community work) in 1980 also helped to give direction and coherence to what had hitherto been a fragmented set of community-based activities. Now, of the three assistant directors, one has responsibility for Community Services. The department lists as two of its five major functions 'the development of services for supporting within the community families with problems, the physically handicapped, the mentally handicapped, the elderly, etc.' and, more significantly, 'through the development of community activities and the stimulation of co-operation with voluntary agencies, the encouragement to use the total resources of the community'. Consonant with these objectives, of the department's expenditure of £22.2 million in 1984/85, 36 per cent went under the heading of Community Support.

The Community Services section does not define its primary responsibility as being to deliver social services. Indeed, the breadth of its approach is shown by the fact that it operates a welfare-rights service to deal with the impact of poverty on vulnerable groups and individuals within the community. Its aim is rather to identify, through its 12 community development workers and their close involvement with the PATs, what issues local people themselves consider significant, to which the department could make an appropriate response. Recognising the danger of 'colonising' people through social work, the section has tried to help and encourage local communities to take responsibility, jointly with the department, for managing neighbourhood projects. It has a reputation for being more ready than most of the council's departments to share information, and the officers of an adjacent department commented favourably upon its concern to devolve power to the neighbourhoods and upon the fact that its field officers understood community work principles.

The staff of 12 work in several localities, in association with local offices which also offer an income-maintenance advisory service. The grant-aid budget through which local organisations can be supported had been pre-empted by older, established voluntary organisations like the council for voluntary service, the citizens advice bureau and the NSPCC which were 'middle class and philanthropic in origin'. However, the problem of funding new activities under increasingly stringent financial constraints has led to the grant-aid policy being reassessed. As a result, the balance has evidently shifted in favour of community groups and newer voluntary organisations, like Women's Aid,

which are concerned with issues which had hitherto been financed not by grant aid but by Inner City Partnership
funds, under Section 11 of the Local Government Act 1972.
The department encourages such groups to apply for support in
order to employ community workers in joint projects designed to
deal with major social needs. These include three health projects
operating under independent committees.

Since this policy of promoting locally-managed projects responds to local circumstances and possibilities, its effectiveness
varies from area to area. Though by no means the first project of
its kind in the city, the Community Project in Scotswood, a
run-down, socially deprived riverside ward, is a particularly interesting case of a locally-managed project. When the Scotswood
Tenants' Association was set up in 1976, it made a bid for Urban
Aid support. Though the local authority at first rejected it, for
fear of encouraging further issue-based campaigning on the
estate, it was eventually accepted with an establishment of two
community workers, a welfare rights worker and, later on, a
'money matters' worker. The tenants' association was run mainly
by local women, who comprised three-quarters of the committee, most of whom had no previous experience of such activity;
and it was they who insisted that these workers should be under
their control and not the council's. Consequently, while the
department covers the project's running costs, responsibility for
policy lies with the Project Management Committee to which
the workers are 'directly accountable and responsible'; and while
the department remains formally responsible for appointments,
the *Responsibility Document* expressly states that the selection of
staff will be a *joint* responsibility, under a locally-elected chairperson.

The project's purposes are 'to improve the living conditions of
people resident in Scotswood e.g., by bringing together tenants'
associations and other voluntary community organisations in a
common effort' and 'to control and support the activities of the
workers who are seconded to the project . . .' In promoting
these aims, the project has continued to organise campaigns for
better housing and social amenities, such as play schemes, while
also promoting a local festival, a credit union (which operates as
a separate organisation), and the Scotswood Employment Project. It also brought pressure to bear to have a redundant school
turned to use as a centre for youth work, adult education and
local employment – the John Marley Centre, as it became in

1984 – and set up working parties to work out the details. Finally, the influence of the women on the project led to a women's health group and a cleaning co-operative being set up, while their demand for a crèche also induced the local authority to allocate a small sum of money for this purpose and to recognise the importance of making this kind of provision more widely. However, the Community Services section's approach was not easily understood in a department largely devoted to social work, so that it took three or four years before the Area Office accepted that the Scotswood Community Project, though financed by their own department, far from being simply another voluntary organisation which could be called upon to help them deal with their clients' problems, was an independent agency with its own rather different brief.

The section's commitment to community development has clearly helped these neighbourhoods a good deal. But its greatest success may well have been to have persuaded social workers to change their ideas about their function, by considering first not what they should be doing for their clients but how they could respond to the issues which the local people considered important and then helping them to manage those projects for themselves. Even so, the community workers may have missed opportunities of working even more effectively with local people by having been concerned with more general issues, like race relations and equal opportunities, which the people in the deprived neighbourhoods themselves did not regard as particularly important and for which councillors would have been reluctant to provide additional resources.

The Youth and Community Service

This joint service, set up just before the new local government structure was introduced in 1974, brought together two hitherto separate functions, the more strongly established Youth Service and the provision of community centres. The section has tried to encourage local people to participate in defining the needs of their communities by being actively involved in the meetings of the Priority Area Teams and by holding frequent discussions with youth and community groups and the voluntary organisations which are represented on the Youth and Community Recreation Sub-Committee. Moreover, the section, often together with the PATs, has helped local communities to assume responsibility for managing social facilities. As a result, the number of small, voluntary community centres and local groups which the section supports has increased fourfold in the past 12 years.

The section has also nurtured the principle of local management, a significant aspect of the community movement's tradition, whereby community centres are managed by their own community associations. This principle has been continued in the newly-established centres, whether local authority or voluntary, and, as far as possible, in the local authority's youth centres, where management committees have also been set up. The City Centre Youth Project, for example, in 1978, was a voluntary project with its own management committee to which two youth workers were seconded. There has accordingly been a long-standing practice of supporting an independent voluntary sector, both in community centres and the associations which have been set up to run them, and in the Youth Service as well.

However, this general principle varies somewhat in its application. All community centres are run by locally-elected committees. But while local authority centres, whose operating costs are fully covered by the council, are managed with the advice and support of a worker by the authority, the independent centres, which cover 50 per cent of their own costs, themselves employ the workers using the city council's grant. Youth centre committees, on the other hand, comprise local councillors and officers, together with laymen 'with an interest in the service of youth'. As they are appointed by the council, they are much more under the department's direct control.

The section has also sought to encourage community associations more effectively to meet the educational and social needs of their communities. In this, they are at a disadvantage compared with the fully-financed Scotswood Community Project since many of them have to raise part of their income as well as manage their centres, an obligation which often inhibits their outreach into the community. Nevertheless, this has sometimes proved practicable, notably at Simonside, where the centre, located in a vast housing development, has been encouraging women on low incomes to discuss their common problems, such as health, social conditions and the level of social security benefits, and has offered them facilities for minding their children and for training in personal skills. Such activities are more likely to have been encouraged by the area-based youth and community workers who are more involved in dealing with local issues than by those who are based in the centres, who tend to see their responsibilities in more restricted terms.

In defining its distinctive function, the Youth and Community Section is particularly concerned to emphasise the fact that its workers have had a professional training in educational or community development roles. This, it is argued, makes them sensitive to problems of community dynamics, which is essential in meeting the difficulties and frustrations which promoting local initiatives can often entail.

The Community Recreation Division

This issue of training has become particularly important since 1983, when the Youth and Community Service was linked with Community Recreation under the Youth and Community Recreation Services Joint Committee. This followed a policy review which suggested that, since a community development approach had been adopted in the field of recreation, the youth and community centres on the one hand and play provision and sports facilities on the other were sufficiently similar for them to be brought together under one joint committee. But this amalgamation also reflects the fact that, until the recent appointment of a new Director of Education, youth and community work had a relatively low standing in the Education Department (which, significantly, only refers to it in the *Introduction* to the City Council's work by noting a reduction in its budget) and the fact that community education is only a small part of a department much larger than Leisure and Recreation, in which 'community recreation' is therefore relatively more prominent.

This enforced collaboration has been based upon the rather superficial view that these two sections make similar kinds of provision for different social needs. But it has ignored their much more fundamental differences of approach. Thus, while the Recreation Department's prime role is to provide amenities for the general public, but under its control, the Youth and Community Service has always sought to encourage the users to manage community and youth centres for themselves, as part of its broader educational philosophy. Certainly, it has not been as successful in doing this in youth centres as in community centres; while the Recreation Department has also been encouraging community organisations to be more fully involved in sports centres and play-groups. Nevertheless, the differences of approach to what community development means continues to provoke disagreements between them.

The Community Recreation Service was set up, after the appointment of a new director, in 1980, in order to encourage people to articulate local needs and to help manage local facilities. By adding responsibility for 'elements of community work' to the work of over a dozen community recreation officers and play-workers, and by appointing a recreation development officer, efforts have been made to involve the voluntary sector in play and recreational provision, to encourage local initiatives and to set up local committees and user-groups to advise on, if not to manage local facilities. Jointly with the Youth and Community Service, 'play forums' have been set up in each ward and local representatives have been consulted about how recreational activities could be more effectively supported in fields ranging from whippet-racing to trampolining. They have encouraged local initiatives and involvement in play-schemes and offered grant aid to sporting organisations and play-groups to employ people and to manage sports centres in various parts of the city. Finally, training courses are helping local people to be more effective leaders in these sports centres and children's play-schemes. It is clear, then, that this section is trying to become much more responsive to local demands and to relate its activities more effectively to the neighbourhoods.

However, this is not easy to achieve in a service which, as its senior officers recognise, 'remains highly facility and task oriented', which is 'constrained by many traditional practices, health and safety regulations and [by] the preconceived views of the Service by the public', and in which simply managing recreational facilities takes up a lot of staff time. It also takes time for the public to become more aware of the opportunities for participation and to change their perceptions of how the leisure service operates. Thus, while it has been relatively easy to get people involved in running play-schemes, this has been much more difficult, though not impossible, in the management of swimming pools. Nor are the local sports centre committees more than advisory bodies. For while the managers may adapt their style to new expectations, the fact that the committee members change fairly frequently ensures that it is the managers who actually control the centres. Indeed, at one sports centre the possibility of replacing the management committee with a users' forum has been considered.

Furthermore, the department is learning about the problems involved in community work. Professional staff can organise

recreation so efficiently, for example, that they can easily discourage people's own involvement; voluntary groups may easily
become so dependent upon the local authority's support that
they cease to generate funds of their own; and inexperienced
groups in particular may be totally discouraged if enthusiastic
officers organise activities for them rather than having the
patience to encourage the people to organise for themselves.
Thus, with only a limited understanding of community work and
very little community development expertise to call on, the
department's activities in this field have been described as
'cosmetic'. Their effect has mainly been, helpfully but in a
limited measure, to have made its operations more 'user-
friendly'. It is nevertheless increasingly aware that its staff require more effective training to undertake this kind of work
properly.

General evaluation

Community development officers in Newcastle were very candid
in acknowledging the limitations of their work. Nevertheless,
the city council in these several ways has made considerable
efforts to develop its work in, and in association with the neighbourhoods. The rethinking which more than ten years' work has
provoked has led to some limited changes in how it is organised.
Community development work has been consolidated in the
Community Services section of the Social Services Department,
a Community Recreation Division has been set up in the Leisure
and Recreation Department, a Youth and Community Recreation Services Joint Committee has been established and the
criteria for grant aid to voluntary organisatons have been clari-
fied. A review of community work by a joint officer group under
the aegis of the Joint Committee has also raised the question of
whether any further reorganisation is necessary.

In the course of these discussions, a useful classification was
suggested which recognises the variety of activities that are
carried out under the heading of community development; activities that range along a continuum from local authority provision to community or neighbourhood control and which we have
already referred to in chapter 2. This pluralistic scheme – what
we will call 'the Newcastle continuum' – in effect legitimises
these very varied activities by incorporating them all under a
common heading of 'community development'. This helpful,
though rather bland framework, however, takes no account of

the real issues which community development work provokes in a local authority. For shifting the balance away from the local authority's direct provision of community services towards community control clearly involves reformulating its functions; and this, while it does not affect its statutory powers, does require some readjustment to its conventional practice as the provider of local services.

The tension between this conventional practice and the further extension of community development does not show up at all in the first few steps along the continuum. In Newcastle, it is recognised that the provision of services must be sensitively attuned to local needs and opinion, so that consulting and involving local groups in its administration is generally taken for granted. In the Priority Area Teams, an innovatory and effective mechanism for consulting local opinion has been evolved. However, some councillors regard even this minor measure of consultation as infringing upon their role and status, even when the decisions are entirely in their hands and when their formal standing as channels of communication with the city council has been expressly safeguarded.

Rather more problematic is their attitude to community action and the few examples of community control. Some exponents of community development among the council's staff consider that the test of the authority's commitment to community development lies in its attitude to these matters. Community workers have occasionally found themselves at odds, if not in conflict with the local authority. This is because if a local community's demand for responsibility is taken seriously, then it is to that *local* group that community workers must make themselves accountable. This can lead members to fear that community workers are nothing more than trouble-makers who are usurping their role; and certainly there is sometimes a conflict of interest between workers and the authority which employs them. Councillors, for example, were annoyed when community workers whom the council employed became actively involved in demonstrating for an Asian women's centre; and workers have had to be dissuaded by their departments from taking too public a part in local campaigns which have been critical of council policy. They have had to learn to be sensitive to the politics of their own positions if they are to resolve the tension inherent in the fact that they have a brief for encouraging local groups to criticise and make claims against the city council which is also their employer.

None the less, the constitution of the Scotswood Community Project demonstrates that local control is perfectly possible without disturbing either the councillor's role or the local authority's prerogatives and responsibilities. It also shows that this degree of decentralisation encourages a high level of participation within the community which has been beneficial for the development of local services. The Byker Advice Centre is also operating under a similar constitution which has been extended to three health projects as well. These projects are all under the Social Services Department which is perhaps the most innovative and adventuresome in this field. But even in the Scotswood project, the question of whether, under its constitution, a department might veto a staff appointment made by the management committee has recently called into question the degree to which that committee is autonomous.

Thus, throughout the system tensions are present between the concepts of representative and participatory democracy. Participatory democracy calls for a good deal of political *nous*, of sensitivity to what it is likely to be politically acceptable for a council employee to do. This has been essential in the Priority Area Teams, where relatively junior officers have dealt with senior local councillors much more directly than is customary for officers of their standing. Such sensitivity is not always found among community workers who sometimes talk big about 'politics' while acting with a singular lack of political finesse. Further, though they may talk about the local community as their sole source of legitimacy, by claiming to be dealing with broader, structural issues, they sometimes stand in danger of manipulating those communities in the interest of their wider political commitments.

These are problems with which any council working in this field is bound to be concerned. That community development is approached in so many different ways in Newcastle upon Tyne means that the several sections of the city council are moving along the community development path at different speeds, according to their particular dispositions and attitudes. This pluralism is a strength rather than a weakness which is appropriate given the highly innovatory nature of this field and the exemplary way in which the city council is exploring and supporting it.

8 From Community Provision to Community Partnership

Interesting and even impressive though some of the developments are which we have described, community development is still a concern of only a minority of local authorities in England and Wales. Granted, not all the authorities which are working in this field replied to our inquiry; but even if they had done so, it would not have affected that conclusion. Even among those which did reply, most had taken only relatively small steps along the Newcastle continuum. While most had accepted that they should consult with voluntary organisations and community groups, only a small number had tried to co-opt them to support the local authorities' own practice, still fewer to encourage community management or community action, and still fewer again community control. Community development therefore is still an unexplored field of work for most local authorities.

Nor is this a matter for surprise. Local government, like central, is chartered first and foremost to provide services for its citizens and to provide them efficiently. In the first instance, it is the responsibility of the elected members to ensure that local opinion is sounded and represented in administrative decisions. Even though only a minority of the electorate votes in local elections, the councillors alone can claim to have a mandate from the electorate as a whole; and they alone are finally responsible for the expenditure of public funds. This view of local government is not to be taken lightly. It is essential that public provision should be made for social needs that cannot be met by individuals acting alone and that the locus of responsibility for that provision should be clear. But this has led to the rather conventional doctrine that the council, and only the council, should provide those public services; and it is this doctrine that has tended to make local authorities reluctant to devolve respon-

sibility more widely. This largely accounts for the relatively slow spread of community development practice. For community development depends upon the acceptance of a pluralistic concept of democracy – the idea that responsibility and initiative should be spread as far as possible among a plurality of institutions within our society.

This pluralistic approach does not in any way question the importance, even the primacy of the formal machinery of government in providing public services. But it does recognise that the government is not the only agency that is, or should be concerned for the public welfare. This is slowly coming to be understood by many local authorities. A booklet on leisure policy produced by the New Forest District Council, for example, expressly states that 'we [the Council] are just one of a large number of organisations that help to provide for leisure in the District . . . We recognise that the great majority of organisations providing for leisure are voluntary and they are the backbone of much that goes on.' In developing its concept of community support, Arun District Council also recognises that it is only one agency among many: 'If the various strands of a community programme are to work then agreement and co-operation with the voluntary agencies is essential.' Such explicit statements, which underpin the practice of many other local authorities which are involved in community development, reflect a pluralistic conception of local democracy, in which the role of local government is not only to provide services directly but to promote partnerships, notably with the voluntary sector, to make that provision still more effective.

'Local government,' the Bains report stated, 'is not, in our view, limited to the narrow provision of a series of services to the local community . . . It has within its purview the overall economic, cultural and physical well-being of the community.' It is concerned more widely with improving living conditions in its locality. This is clear enough in the economic sphere, where the economic vitality of a town may well depend upon the local council's ability to set the conditions which will encourage employers to establish their works and their offices there. By the same token, local councils can also determine the conditions which may encourage, rather than discourage other groups or organisations within their area to make their contribution to the community life of the town. Local government, accordingly, has a function not only to provide services but to establish the conditions that favour, rather than inhibit, the contributions which voluntary organisations have to make. That is the central meaning of community development.

The voluntary sector

The voluntary sector, from the standpoint of a local authority, often appears amorphous and confusing. This is because it consists of a large number of different kinds of organisation which are mostly independent of each other and differently constituted. They are 'voluntary' in the sense that they are neither statutory nor commercial, and that, while they may well employ staff, they also engage the services of unpaid, volunteer workers. It was in the first sense of the term that, before the Second World War, many hospitals were described as 'voluntary'. In much the same way that those hospitals in 1948 became part of the National Health Service so, it was often thought, would other voluntary welfare organisations disappear, as their functions were incorporated in the Welfare State. Far from this being the case, the fact is that the range of voluntary organisations has steadily grown in the course of the past 40 years.

From the earlier period there remain particularly the large, nationally-organised voluntary bodies such as the National Society for the Prevention of Cruelty to Children and the British Red Cross, which embody an older, and at one time rather patronising charitable tradition of concern for the welfare of others. Other national organisations such as Relate – formerly the Marriage Guidance Council – and the National Children's Bureau can now be added to that distinguished list. Then there are the bodies like councils for voluntary service or the rural community councils which, started after the First World War, have burgeoned since the end of the last war as general support and development agencies for the voluntary sector. A further very significant development in recent years has been the very rapid growth of all manner of small, local voluntary groups which have been set up to promote particular causes. Many of these are self-help groups which have been formed by people facing problems – Gingerbread, the organisation for single parents, for example – to give each other support in their common difficulties and to organise themselves to protect and to campaign for their own interests. Tenants' and residents' associations have a similar function. Other local organisations have also come into existence not so much to meet difficulties as to promote social, educational and cultural causes: community associations, educational centres, village colleges, civic groups, sporting clubs and musical festivals. All these, taken together, constitute the 'voluntary sector': organisations which, though they sometimes employ a small salaried staff, are mostly run without payment by ordinary people acting as members of their local communities.

The value of these organisations for the well-being of a community can best be illustrated in the field of social welfare. A recent study of the 26 voluntary welfare organisations which Thamesdown Borough Council grant aided in 1982/83 showed that their value amounted to £1.25 million. This was made up of the £750,000 which it cost them to provide accommodation, staff and administrative support, plus an estimated £500,000 which would have been the *minimum* cost of the voluntary help given to them if it had had to be paid for. This figure of £1.25 million was 20 per cent of the operating costs of the county council's Social Services Department in this one district. The voluntary sector accordingly added a fifth to the social services provision in the town. To this £1.25 million, the ratepayers of the district contributed about £320,000, in the ratio two-fifths from the borough (£129,000) and three-fifths from the county. The remaining £930,000 came from central government, charitable trusts, clients' fees and fund raising, but with the largest single contribution, equivalent in value to £0.5 million, coming from the freely-given work of voluntary workers. Thus, the borough council contributed roughly one pound for every ten to this supplementary social service: a very good return indeed.

This quantitative analysis, however, needs to be supplemented by other, qualitative observations. In Thamesdown, these voluntary organisations provide a range of advisory services such as a marriage guidance bureau, a citizens advice bureau and a law centre; round-the-clock services for people in difficulties, such as the Samaritans or Gingerbread; large numbers of pre-school play-groups; and so on. Moreover, the service which these voluntary bodies provides is quite distinctive. Because they are largely run by unpaid volunteers, they are able, for example, to make available one helper for every single handicapped child who uses the hydro-therapy pool, which it would be well beyond the resources of the statutory authority to offer. An organisation like Gingerbread or the Samaritans can operate a 24-hour all-round-the-year service for people facing emergencies or distress. In many similar organisations, the service is given by people who, unlike most social workers, have themselves been through the traumas with which their clients now have to deal. As Kipling put it, only 'The toad beneath the harrow knows/Exactly where each tooth-point goes'; and people facing such difficulties are more likely to overcome their problems and regain their shattered self-respect if they are supported by others who have themselves faced similar adversities. This continuing social support is a bonus whose value cannot easily be costed but which cannot be ignored.

In such organisations, but equally in the other voluntary bodies that are concerned not with social problems but with promoting sociability or sporting, educational or cultural activities, the value of voluntary action can be clearly seen. But, in a still wider sense, their value rests upon the fact that they not only provide a service within their communities but that they do so in a quite distinctive manner. For voluntary organisations are, first, self-governing bodies which are run directly by their own members; which, second, operate on the principle of self-help, providing from within their own membership the stimulus, the drive, the labour and very often the funds that are needed to offer a service to the community; and, which, third, activate the potential for social action within their communities, so that these contributions can be made. In this sense, then, the voluntary sector is an essential and desirable part of any society that claims to be a democracy and which seeks to encourage initiative and responsibility among its citizens. Community development in local authorities, then, is concerned with fostering partnerships with the voluntary bodies and community groups which constitute that sector.

Local authorities and community development

Increasingly in recent years, local authorities up and down the country have started to recognise the value and importance of this communal potential, so that the term 'community development' has entered the vocabulary of local government, though there is some uncertainty about what it means. Local authorities begin community development for a variety of reasons. One of the earliest stimuli was the recognition that people needed places in which to meet and hold social functions, in rural villages no less than in the new housing estates where, between the wars, the 'community spirit' of the slums was generally thought to be lacking. Schemes of grant aid were accordingly introduced to enable village halls and community centres to be erected. The principle of grant aiding voluntary organisations was extended in rural areas under the former Development Commission, to rural community councils and, under other arrangements to councils of social service in urban districts, both of them 'umbrella organisations' serving and supporting voluntary organisations. The equally important principle of self-management was primarily endorsed in the community associations which, in many areas, had taken on responsibility for running community centres. After the Second World War, in the new and expanding towns and in new housing estates, many authorities like Swindon began community development out of a concern to help their new residents settle in their new environments.

From these strands, community development has grown into the wide variety of activities that have been considered in the previous chapters. It has often spread to other local authorities as a result of external pressure. Central government programmes, however, such as Urban Aid and the Manpower Services Commission's Community Programme, though they have frequently been used to finance community development projects, especially in underprivileged communities, do not appear to have led the authorities that have used them to adopt community development more generally. More effective in doing so has been the Community Projects Foundation (CPF), an organisation mainly funded by the Home Office, which for 20 years has been promoting community development projects in association with local authorities. But even if these initiatives have not induced local councils to continue work of this kind themselves, they have certainly helped in many areas to make community development better known and understood.

Direct example appears to have had more effect. When local authorities were amalgamated into larger districts in 1974, the newly-constituted authorities sometimes took on a community development function that had previously been a feature of one of their constituent authorities. Hereford and Worcester's involvement grows from Herefordshire's prior commitment to this field, which itself grew out of the CPF's Leominster project in the 1970s. Kirklees, again, acknowledges the influence of the former Batley Corporation in its present-day policy towards community associations. Other authorities, such as Northampton, Redditch and Warrington, on which New Town Development Corporations had been superimposed, continued the community development work which many of these corporations had promoted, though often with far fewer resources. Redditch, for instance, having taken over the physical amenities that the corporation had provided, soon came to realise that it also had to continue its community development work as well. Similarly in Warrington, where over the past decade the town has been transformed, 'it has become apparent that physical development alone does not lead to social well being'. Faced with increasing social stress and unemployment, larger numbers of elderly people, drug taking, vandalism and homelessness, and with the Development Corporation about to be wound up, the council has decided to establish a community development service of its own.

The increasingly stringent economic contraints within which local authorities have had to operate in recent years have also obliged them to consider the cost-effectiveness of their services. Many of them have come to recognise that voluntary organisations and community groups are real resources which could contribute very beneficially to their services. This has meant collaborating with, and supporting these organisations, as has been done in Lincolnshire and elsewhere, or co-opting the voluntary sector to supplement their own activities, especially in social work. It has also added force to their concern to bring their services more effectively into contact with their clientèle. Social services departments, for example, have been encouraged to devolve their work onto neighbourhood teams; leisure and recreation departments have sought to relate to local communities by promoting play-groups and informal recreational activities; community education has meant, at the least, making school premises more readily available for local use; housing departments have been obliged to relate more closely to their tenants. The result of individual authorities' initiatives in the first place, these developments have been encouraged by national reports, national bodies and sometimes legislation, the response to which has varied with the attitudes, personnel and policies of each local authority, with different departments taking the leading roles.

This more demanding pattern of financial control has also afforded many local authorities an additional justification for giving priority to disadvantaged groups, such as unemployed people and ethnic minorities. Community development in this context has been a method for redistributing resources to them and for encouraging them to organise themselves to meet their special needs. Thus many authorities, such as Birmingham and Leeds, have set up local economic development agencies, expressly to benefit 'the most disadvantaged members of the community' who are generally the most difficult groups both to relate to and to encourage, and for whom community development appears to offer a particularly helpful method of work. In Deeside, where the closing of the Shotton steelworks in 1979 resulted in the largest scale of redundancy in Western Europe, Clwyd County Council, helped to organise the Deeside Community Agency 'to support local people and initiatives' in dealing with some of the social problems which this brought about.

How these several factors affect local authorities varies with their particular circumstances. But in many cases it is clear that particular members and officers have been responsible for moving their authorities to adopt a community development approach. This was particularly clear in the account of Cambridge in chapter 5, where one officer was noted as having encouraged the residents' association, the success of the community service team was ascribed to the enthusiasm of another and where the community and welfare initiative had been promoted by one councillor especially who had been impressed by a similar scheme in Harlow, where he worked. There can be no doubt that other individuals have played similar roles in many other authorities.

Nevertheless, so much more depends, as our examples have shown, upon the general attitude of the authority and the degree to which its senior officers and members are committed to community development. Many officers stress the importance of this factor. In Northampton, the future development of the residents' councils depended 'ultimately on the commitment of the NDC or the local authority to resident participation itself'. A Peterborough report commented, in a similar vein, that the city's new approach to community development 'will not be fully effective unless a dialogue is created and maintained at a more senior officer level and in certain circumstances at member level, to ensure that sufficient support can be given at the 'sharp end' of service delivery'. Islington's report on decentralisation equally noted that progress had depended upon collaboration among the chairmen of committees, the maintenance of political pressure for change and the fact that the officers' working group could keep up the pressure on chief officers to keep things moving. The growth of community development in Newcastle upon Tyne, as in Thamesdown, owes a great deal to alliances that were created between the political leaders and several sympathetic and committed senior officers, while in Cambridge, as in many other authorities, this kind of work commands support (no doubt for slightly different reasons) from both sides of the council chamber. It may be significant that the style of the officers in both Newcastle and Thamesdown was described as 'free and open' and 'candid'.

As for political alignment, a third of all the authorities which replied were controlled by the Conservatives. These included authorities like Arun and Hereford and Worcester which have developed exemplary community development schemes. While there was no appreciable difference in the scale of staffing in community development as between Labour and Conservative county councils, Labour-controlled district councils, as compared with Conservative ones, had significantly larger staffs. This is consistent with the fact that they also spent more per head on local services (£74 against £52), probably because they had relatively dense populations in which social need was a good deal more pronounced.

Towards a community development policy

The replies which we received to our inquiry indicated that, among the authorities active in this field, a good deal of positive rethinking was being done about how they should organise community development. New appointments were being planned, new committees set up, new activities started: fascinating evidence of vitality. In particular, many authorities were beginning to realise that they needed to set community development within a wider framework of thinking, and thus of policy. This arose partly from functional considerations, partly from a recognition that practical difficulties were often brought about through failing to think about the principles on which community development should best be organised. Sometimes, community development work had been introduced in one department which had slowly come to see that a more coherent departmental policy needed to be worked out. In other cases, notably in larger authorities such as Birmingham, similar initiatives had been taken in a number of different departments – setting up community councils, encouraging community associations, introducing the dual use of school buildings, decentralising the social services – and the authority was beginning to consider whether, and how it might devise a general community development policy.

The desirability of doing so was brought out by several authorities which had run into difficulties through not having done so. In the London Borough of Hounslow, a report on the council's relationship with the 22 community and residents' associations which it supported financially indicated some of the problems that had arisen, perhaps because of 'a more general lack of overall direction in the application of resources and adoption of systems for encouragement of community development'. For example, it had discovered that, under their constitutions, the council was not represented on an association's governing body and therefore had no right to monitor, still less to intervene in their affairs early enough to avert the difficulties which had sometimes arisen in running them or to prevent their total collapse. In Ealing, again, it was suggested that the various ways in which different departments consulted the public could easily lead to public consultation being discredited through inconsistencies in information or procedures. Badly managed efforts at consultation could easily become mere 'complaint sessions', dominated by people who were highly motivated and articulate to the detriment of the more deprived and less articulate. They could equally 'show up the inadequacies of the same department or other complementary services, and thus consolidate residents' worst suspicions – that the local authority is secretive, inefficient and unresponsive'. For all these reasons, a more coherent policy was thought desirable.

A more general reason why local authorities should think out such a policy is clearly drawn out in a Tameside report on community education. This notes judiciously:

The resources available to the Authority are clearly not sufficient to allow it to respond to the need for community [sic] as it would like. Indeed one of the paradoxes of successful community education work is that it tends to emphasise the degree of shortfall as needs become more clearly identified.

Even councillors and officers who are sympathetic to community development may well feel anxious that, if they are not careful, they may be putting their fingers into a hornets' nest of trouble or opening a Pandora's box of demands for more and more re-sources, at a time when resources are severely curtailed. They may also suspect that the councillors' own position might be undermined by encouraging another system of representation through local community activists

These considerations are real enough; and organisations which, like the National Coalition, wish to encourage local authorities to adopt community development must take them seriously. Local authorities entering this field of activity should therefore be careful to anticipate the kind of issues and problems which we now turn to consider. They should develop coherent policies that balance the claims and expectations of community groups with the more general concerns and obligations of which the authority itself is the guardian. That these problems need not constitute insuperable difficulties is clear from the practice of those authorities which have successfully moved in this direction and whose experience and thinking have been drawn upon throughout this book.

Starting principles

To develop coherent and consistent policies for relating to voluntary and community organisations, however, must not re-sult in local authorities' trying to standardise them. Whereas statutory organisations have a fairly standard pattern of organisation and clearly defined functions, voluntary organisations are much more idiosyncratic and varied. Thus, they may be located randomly, depending much more upon particular local circumstances and often upon the fortuitous presence of a particular leader. In the western part of Arun, for example, the voluntary sector was more effectively organised through the Bognor Regis CVS than it was in the east of the district, while 20 years ago, the community care groups which are now found all over Hampshire were almost all located along the coast. But more locally-based community organisations are even more volatile. As many authorities have noted, some with a tone of slight exasperation, bodies such as tenants' and community associations 'tend to wax and wane in their levels of activity and periodically collapse altogether'. The residents' councils in Northampton, for example, were variously 'dogged' by internal disputes, and sometimes 'unsure about the direction they should take', while the disruptive effects were noted of 'the very high level of mobility of members moving away from the area', of key members who had to resign for family reasons and who could not easily be replaced, and of organisations where 'it had been impossible to attract sufficient people wishing to hold office'.

This last point is particularly important, since it does not follow that local people always share the same degree of enthusiasm for participating in local organisations as the more committed exponents of participation often expect. In Northampton itself, the residents evidently did not wish their councils to assume managerial responsibilities or to become housing co-operatives, as the Development Corporation had once thought possible. Nor did the voluntary organisations in Thamesdown, despite the generally favourable atmosphere, appear to have sought any wider influence on the borough's general policy.

Nevertheless, the residents' councils in Northampton were encouraged to extend their concerns from housing to general environmental issues, on the grounds that more broadly based councils with wider responsibilities were more likely to be successful. Indeed, it seems to be generally accepted that the effectiveness of local representative bodies is likely to be greater the more real responsibility they command. The community development officer in Hereford and Worcester put the point succinctly in saying that 'when local people feel that their efforts can make a difference, they will participate'. The Harlow working party considered that 'if neighbourhood committees were to be successful then they needed to have real power and should not simply be consultative bodies'. Tameside, again, stated that its community education forums would be 'weak, ill-attended and unproductive' if they did not have 'substantial responsibilities and powers'. Though these propositions are statements of belief rather than validated conclusions, they seem plausible enough to justify accepting them as at least provisionally valid.

Certainly, many local authorities have been willing to give local voluntary and community organisations quite tangible responsibilities. In response to the frequent comments from members of the public that the proposed community councils in Hounslow 'should be given the power to determine local policy otherwise they would [merely] become a talking shop', it was stated that they would each have a budget of probably £50,000 – 70,000 to allocate. In Islington, local officials were expected to act on the recommendations of the neighbourhood councils unless they were illegal or contravened council policy. Even so, it is also clear that the public will need encouraging to accept responsibility, especially in local representative bodies. Islington recognised that 'the public needed convincing that they would have real influence and that their views would be taken seriously'; that the neighbourhood forums 'will not evolve overnight'; and that much effort would be needed 'to draw in people who have not been used to expressing their views in this way'. Harlow likewise commented that 'it is unlikely that people will come forward spontaneously to take part in the new structures immediately they are set up' and that initially 'directly elected representatives will be lacking in experience, and there may be very few community groups which are based on the neighbourhood'.

Work with local community groups, which are often rather less formally constituted than voluntary organisations, may require even more care and patience. For whereas some communities may be sufficiently experienced and competent in running organisations to be able to take responsibility for their own affairs from the outset, others may need considerable help in learning to do so. These will often be in deprived and underprivileged neighbourhoods which are sometimes at a disadvantage in representing their own local interests. Community work of this kind is invariably (as a worker in Middlesbrough accurately described it) 'a slow, painstaking process, punctuated by some setbacks'. But this must be accepted since the local authority is not providing a

service but encouraging democratic practice, a process which demands the patience of the educator rather than the efficiency of the administrator. As the chief executive of Hounslow states in a report on community associations, '. . . the Council's main role is to facilitate rather than direct. Associations will always be subject to upheaval and errors of judgement in the conduct of their affairs and *this is part of the community learning process* [our italics].'

The care that is needed in this process is well illustrated in the development of community associations. Like many other authorities, Hull has recognised that community buildings may remain empty 'without the encouragement of good practice . . . or be mistreated as initial enthusiasm and willingness to co-operate wanes in the face of mounting managerial problems.' Accordingly, like Scunthorpe, it carefully monitors the phases by which local groups eventually take over the management of centres. It considers that, however desirable it might be for them to take this responsibility as soon as a centre is opened, this should wait until the community concerned is ready to take it on. Thus, 'the assumption of full management responsibilities by local people may be the outcome of a long-term process rather than its starting point'.

But though local authorities should be sensitive to such factors, which are inevitably involved in the community education process, this should not prevent them adopting clear policies and procedures for community development. In replying to a question about whether his local authority had adopted any policy statement on community development, one officer stated: 'Never! Our policy is to be flexible, imaginative, catalysts creating bridges where needed between authority and volunteers etc.' These are virtues which community development certainly needs. But they need to be related to clear standards of practice. As another authority rightly put it, 'the Council, in making a financial commitment to community activity, has a public duty to ensure that certain minimum standards are met.' In insisting on these, a local authority is also acting in the best interests of the voluntary sector.

Economic considerations

Clearly, any local authority thinking of starting or expanding community development is bound to be concerned with how much it will cost. A small inquiry like this obviously cannot determine precisely what balance of costs and benefits would be entailed in any particular case, for circumstances vary in each locality and according to what kind of development is envisaged. Even a local council interested in decentralising its services might not wish, still less be able to find the £10 million which Islington expects will be the capital cost of its operation or to add over 100 new staff to its establishment. Nor does it need to in order to make some headway in this field.

Much will hang upon the council's general approach. A report in Halton six years ago stated that 'when there is more pressure on local government to monitor its expenditure and set up systems to control the various committee budgets, then the parts charged with promoting new ideas for a more effective service delivery are all but stifled'. These financial constraints have certainly become even more stringent since then; and many proposals that were being brought forward when we started this inquiry two years ago have been halted, or at least reduced in scale. As Eric Adams commented of Southwark,

With such restriction on funds there is a reluctance to widen the community development debate – what is the point of raising people's hopes and ambitions when there are no financial resources to meet them? There are so many problems on the current agenda that there is no general eagerness to start more restructuring or debate which could only exacerbate issues which already weigh heavily enough within departments. Past experience of both corporate responsibilities/cross departmental initiatives and community involvement do not encourage such risks.

Nevertheless, many other authorities are going ahead with community development projects, notwithstanding these financial difficulties. Though they may have been obliged to put off creating new departments or reorganising them, they are still appointing new staff, starting new projects, while thinking even more carefully about the cost-effectiveness of their proposals. Three years ago, Tameside, for example, accepted that no new funds would be forthcoming for its community education programme and saw that it would have to work more than ever to precise priorities and ensure 'that *all* the resources available are identified, that they are applied in line with objectives and resources without waste, and that they are applied to maximum effect'.

Certainly, the effort to bring services closer to the local users by decentralising them is likely to cost more than retaining a relatively centralised structure. Like campaigns to make citizens more aware of their welfare rights, decentralisation is also likely to increase demands upon the local authority's services. The Islington report notes that 'as anticipated . . . "going local" has led to quite unexpected and unprecedented levels of demand in some neighbourhoods'. This has 'put considerable pressure on operational and administrative staff and has led, in turn, to demands for additional staff, only some of which can be met from the council's limited resources'. This increased demand, however, demonstrates the degree to which the local authority's services were being under-used: and under-used most probably by those relatively disadvantaged members of society, such as old, infirm or unemployed people, who need the service most but may well have found it too inconvenient or too unsympathetic to use. These services accordingly might be said to have become more efficient by having become more responsive to local needs and more cost-effective than they were before. Savings made by improving a service may also offset some of the costs of additional staff.

As for investment in voluntary and community organisations, as a Hereford and Worcester report makes clear, '"self-help" is not "free" help, and some investment will be necessary to release the potential'. Nor will savings follow immediately since 'trying to create a healthy community doesn't instantly remove its immediate problems'. But supporting these organisations has important pay-offs since it capitalises upon the efforts, the energy, the know-how and the sheer hard work of volunteers. In giving financial support to people to manage facilities for themselves, for example, the local authority is not only maximising the use of those resources within the community, it is also encouraging local democracy and self-management, which it is one of the major goals of community development to foster. Slough comments that 'the potential of devolving management responsibility [of a community centre] will be pursued in the expectation that this could bring revenue savings and increase the level of lettings'. Finally, when a local authority supports a voluntary body, that organisation is given a public recognition, which is itself a resource since it is then that much easier for it to argue for additional support from charitable foundations and other agencies. As Hereford and Worcester points out, one of the reasons they could attract outside resources for their Rural Community Development Project was because the funders saw it 'as being a definite commitment on the part of the Local Authority'. Thus, pragmatic, cost-benefit considerations go hand in hand with the more principled desire to encourage community development itself.

A note of caution, however, is needed. It would be understandable if, under conditions of financial stringency, local authorities were only to support community groups which could directly contribute to their own services. A Hampshire discussion paper on criteria for grants to voluntary organisations has suggested that 'the Committee may wish to look to the voluntary sector to provide a specific service which had been identified as required for a client group in a specific area'. The committee, 'instead of simply reacting to a request for a particular initiative . . . can be "pro-active" suggesting developments that they would like to see the voluntary sector coming forward to meet'.

Such a procedure is entirely appropriate. But local authorities ought not to be so pro-active that voluntary bodies are precluded from putting up proposals at *their* initiative for their local councils to support. Voluntary organisations still engage in their traditional role of defining and meeting new needs which the statutory authorities only subsequently acknowledge. Thus, the Family Planning Association, which was developed in the teeth of a great deal of official hostility, maintained a contraceptive service for over forty years which was only taken over by the National Health Service in 1974. The community care groups, which now support the Social Services Department's work in Hampshire, also started as a private initiative at a time when the department had strong reservations about making use of volunteers. This reservation about not pre-empting voluntary initiatives in the interest of functional efficiency applies especially to community groups which may be less well organised than larger voluntary bodies, may be concerned with leisure-time activities rather than social welfare problems, and which may also be more openly critical of the local authority itself.

Changes of style

If a community development policy means increasing staff, this might simply lead to an even larger bureaucracy. The residents of Hounslow, for instance, when consulted about the borough's plans for decentralising its services, frequently expressed their anxiety that to set up neighbourhood offices 'would merely result in adding another link to the existing management chain'. The councillor who was presenting the proposals at public meetings agreed 'that decentralisation would not of itself improve services if it simply transplanted bureaucracy to the local level'. However, he envisaged 'a change of "style" in service delivery making offices more welcoming, and training workers with cross-functional skills which would speed up service delivery'. In short, since community development means closer collaboration between the local authority and voluntary and community groups, then it will require the local authority's officers to adopt a very different style and approach.

Such a readjustment will obviously be much less acute in those departments which regard community development as simply co-opting volunteers or groups to supplement their service. For in that case, though local people are certainly being encouraged to participate, community development is seen simply as a convenient means of supporting one particular service, like social work, to which people are recruited entirely at the local authority's initiative. But when community development is interpreted as encouraging local democracy or self-help and involves setting up community forums or supporting neighbourhood groups, then the central question ceases to be 'what can *we* do for them?' or 'how can they help us?' but 'how can we help *them* to articulate and to meet *their* local needs?'. It means accepting that the local people themselves will be taking the initiative to register complaints and put up proposals, and dealing with local issues in which not just one, but a number of departments and authorities may well be involved.

This approach is very different from the traditional stance of local government which sees its role as being simply to provide a service, of which the citizen is expected to remain a passive, compliant and preferably grateful recipient. Community development, on the other hand, even in providing a community centre, would seek to encourage the people for whom it was being provided to participate in providing and in running it. It would do this by consulting with them, associating them with its design and then advising them about setting up a community association in order to run it for themselves. Community development, at best, is an educational process in which local government, far from simply providing for people's needs, enters into partnership with them to do so. For officers who have spent their careers in offices, assuming that the local authority's sole function is to provide a service, to change to a community partnership style is likely to be neither easy nor congenial.

In the kind of community development work that is concerned with helping communities solve their own problems, since the prime focus is the community itself, it tends to be concerned not just with one particular service but with how the various services and resources relate to one another in that context. This inevitably involves working across conventional administrative boundaries. As the first annual report of the Community Development Unit in Hereford and Worcester states, the central problem is 'how best to integrate existing resources and services to make them more accessible to the community, and how to develop the co-operation needed within and between the organisations who held those resources to release them and help local communities become more self-sufficient.' Likewise in Arun, it is recognised that community support for the frail elderly would require the local authority to collaborate much more closely with both the voluntary sector and the health and social services agencies. This in turn would necessitate 'a change in the general philosophy of this Council and the other agencies' and 'a move towards a more community-based approach . . . and the breaking down of the traditional barriers between housing, grant aid, community services, environmental health, transport, social services, etc.' As a result, to quote the example given in our account of Crewe and Nantwich, 'a Recreation Division employee, working with a neighbourhood group is as likely to be working on issues related to housing provision or welfare rights as he or she is to be working solely in the recreation field.'

Certainly, administrative boundaries may prove difficult to surmount, even in authorities which are sympathetic to community development. Even in Thamesdown, where it has a relatively strong and well-established position, community development is still said to be viewed suspiciously by other departments, while in Newcastle it was sometimes difficult to ensure full collaboration between departments which had adopted rather different approaches to community development itself. In Cambridgeshire, again, even though both the Education and the Social Services departments were planning to decentralise their services, scant reference was made in either department's documentation to the other's proposals. Nevertheless, these problems are not insuperable. Cambridge City and the county council appear to have collaborated effectively in this field and the county officers recognised that they had learnt a good deal from the city team. More significantly, in regard to grant aid for community development projects, which the Crewe and Nantwich report suggested were particularly difficult to arrange, in both Hampshire and Thamesdown unambiguous arrangements have been made under which both county and district councils contribute jointly, and in agreed proportions, to the funding of appropriate voluntary organisations.

A further change of style is called for when officers are expected to deal with members of the public as partners within the more open context of the community, rather than in the restrictive setting of a local authority office. For housing officers in Cambridge, for instance, the first experience of consulting tenants' associations made them feel 'as if their professional skill was being undermined'. Within the voluntary sector, the tendency to retreat into the safety of a building is no less evident. Community associations were originally intended to be both social centres and bases for social action within their communities. But a recent review of their role in Dacorum, confirming evidence from elsewhere, has shown that 'the Associations are preoccupied with managing the centres and they have little involvement with the neighbourhood outside the centre or with other neighbourhood groups despite good intentions'. For however active they may once have been, they are nowadays managed by elderly people who 'lack the necessary skills and vision to make the best use of the centres' and whose excessively cautious attitude inhibits the development of new activities or of reaching out to meet the needs of the wider community.

If voluntary organisations which are chartered to serve the wider community fail to do so, then it is hardly surprising if local government officers, accustomed to providing a service, find it difficult to accommodate to the newer style that is required in community development work. Thus social workers in Newcastle upon Tyne, for example, took several years to accept that a community project which was financed by their department was not simply another organisation which they could call upon for help in dealing with their clients' problems. Indeed, the head of the community services section of that department considered his greatest success to have been to persuade other social workers to consider first, not what they should be doing for their clients, but how they could help their clients to manage self-help projects for themselves. Youth workers and community workers, too, operating in education departments, are often divided by a deep cleft of incomprehension; so much so that Hertfordshire is running down community work and retaining only youth work which is regarded as 'more tangible'. For youth workers, most of whom originally trained as teachers, are accustomed to operating in premises like schools and youth clubs while community workers typically work in the more open context of the local street or the neighbourhood organisation.

In part, the difficulty of reorienting work from the office to the community may be aggravated by the attitudes of the public. In Newcastle upon Tyne, community recreation has been constrained by 'the preconceived views of the Service by the public'. In the same way, community workers in Cambridge who operated from community centres had also been impeded from working more within the wider community because the people who used the centres still regarded them as being primarily responsible for organising activities within the building. That is why neighbourhood workers in Thamesdown avoid using centres as their base.

Community development in the administrative structure

One question which a local authority has to consider in enaging in community development is where, in its administrative structure, it is most appropriately located. Initially at least, this is less likely to be affected by general considerations than by practical, historical and political factors. Understandably, therefore, it tends to be incorporated into an existing department as one aspect of its specialised function. Even though our inquiry does not cover all the authorities that are working in this field, our evidence is probably generally valid. Of the 71 authorities which gave us that information, community development in district councils was mainly located in housing and in leisure and recreation departments, while in counties and metropolitan districts the departments mainly involved were social services and education.

The location of community development within a functional department has the advantage that it enables this new approach to be integrated with minimum strain and disturbance into the local authority's existing framework and ethos. On the other hand, it tends to define community development rather narrowly, as being a kind of appendage to that department's service function rather than as a method of working that has a more general relevance. Thus, even after six years, in 1981, the activities of the Hereford and Worcester rural community development project 'have often been regarded as "Social Services" because two of the people most closely involved are officers of that Department'. This had resulted, especially within the authority, 'in a preconceived and incorrect idea of the kinds of issues the Project was concerned with, and has frequently led to staff in other departments feeling that it was nothing to do with them and had no right to be involved in their specialist areas of concern'. By the same token, if the proposal had been accepted that Thamesdown's Community Development Division should be taken out of the strategically-located Development and Housing Group and relocated in the Arts and Leisure Group, its contribution to the life of the area would probably have been seriously diminished. For, as Stephen Humble noted in Stevenage, the fact that community development was located in the leisure and community services department meant that its more general relevance was blunted by the department's overriding concern for providing facilities. As a result, 'the Department (as a whole) does not set out in any comprehensive manner to stimulate the expression of need by local communities and to try to provide resources to meet these needs'. In other words, in that context, there is little incentive to move towards the more positive ideas that are at the further end of the 'community development continuum'.

If community development is not defined as an adjunct to a service department, the most obvious alternative is to place it, as a central function of the authority, in the Chief Executive's Department. This is particularly important for a function which tends to cut across departmental and other organisational boundaries. This solution is often arrived at when community development has been reviewed in an authority in which a number of different initiatives have been started in this field. Thus Hereford and Worcester, after a general review of the council's community development activities, decided to place the Community Development Unit under the chief executive but to require its activities to be undertaken 'with and through the Council's service departments'. In Newcastle upon Tyne, the Priority Area Teams, which were the city's first community development agencies in deprived neighbourhoods, were taken from the Planning Department and placed eventually in the Chief Executive's Department. In Halton and Clwyd, community development work was similarly located. Finally, in Hounslow, the fact that the borough has variously promoted community councils, community associations, the dual use of schools and developments within the social services has raised the question whether they should remain under the functional departments or be brought together in a separate Community Development Unit, probably under the chief executive.

The value of locating this function in the Chief Executive's Department is clearly brought out in a report from Halton. This location made it possible for the project officers 'to be able to follow any issue into any service of the Council', which was important since most issues in this field affect more than one department. Second, it made it easier for them to get 'essential background information' and to contact members of staff throughout the organisation. Third, it afforded them 'a freedom to act as required without being tied by usual local government procedures'. And finally, it demonstrated publicly that the project 'had the direct support of the Top'.

An alternative practice which gives community development

something of the independence of particular service departments which, in our opinion, it needs is to place it under a separate committee. Thus in Thamesdown, a Community Planning Committee was formed when the local authority was reorganised in 1974 and has become one of the most important committees in the council. Peterborough, again, anticipating the winding-up of Peterborough Development Corporation, has recently appointed a Community Development Sub-Committee which has produced a very thoughtful paper outlining a policy that embodies a very broad view of community development, within the framework of the Leisure and Amenities Committee. But though still under a service department, community development is now being interpreted so as to focus more broadly 'on needs and aspirations as perceived by the community rather than by the local Authority'; and community groups are being supported more directly through a more decentralised service which gives priority to disadvantaged sections of the community, especially ethnic minorities.

Locating community development with the chief executive or placing it under a special committee does not, of course, ensure that this function will be fully accepted within the local authority. In Thamesdown, though community development is generally accepted, this has evidently not prevented other departments viewing it with suspicion; nor have the Priority Area Teams in Newcastle upon Tyne 'had any direct effect upon a committee's decisions, still less influenced directly its spending pattern on policy', as originally had been thought possible. Nevertheless, this process of consolidating community development, either under the aegis of the chief executive or in a separate committee offers this field a definition and, most of all, a recognition that helps establish its credibility. Even where, as in Cambridge, the Community Services Committee only consolidates the authority's existing work, it still gives it credibility since its importance is thereby clearly recognised as a central function of the council.

Political issues
Scepticism about community development arises partly because of its relative novelty and partly because it departs from the traditional concept of the role of local government as being to provide a service towards developing partnerships with the local community. In addition, as one south coast authority sees it, it is

'a vague and wishy-washy kind of thing which cannot be accur-ately measured and tends to be simply trendy, with people rushing to do it so as to be on the bandwagon'. But much more important is the view that many councillors share that commun-ity workers may easily prejudice their relationship with their own constituents by forming, as it were, a secondary system of repre-sentation.

The main issue has to do with the relationship and the balance of interests between the local authority and community groups. A distinction may be drawn between them and voluntary organ-isations. Voluntary organisations, such as Age Concern or a Council for Voluntary Service, are usually more formally organ-ised than community groups; and though they, too, may be badly run, it is more often community groups whose stability is likely to fluctuate. A voluntary organisation, furthermore, is likely to have a much more precisely-defined function than a community group. Consequently, in dealing with voluntary organisations, by offering them grant aid for example, a local authority is more likely to know in advance what use will be made of its support. In some cases, such as the Hampshire community care groups, whose interests are congruent with those of the county council, voluntary organisations are willingly co-opted into supporting the work of the local authority, while the interests of other organisations like Relate may be said to be complementary. At all events, even though such bodies may not always agree with the local authorities which support them, they do not for the most part attack them or criticise their policies too publicly, still less demonstrate and campaign against them.

Community groups, on the other hand, are often highly criti-cal of their local councils. Indeed, tenants' and residents' organ-isations are often set up precisely (and properly) to exert pressure on their councils to improve amenities or to negotiate with them on behalf of their members. Moreover, the range of issues with which a community organisation may be concerned tends to be rather wider than with a single-purpose voluntary organis-ation. Community groups, finally, may need to be supported more directly than voluntary organisations; and local authorities may consider this particularly necessary for groups that represent deprived or disadvantaged communities. Community groups, accordingly, are much more likely to come into conflict with their local authorities.

This propensity may sometimes be aggravated by the role of

community workers who work with these groups and who enjoy the reputation of being stirrers-up of trouble. The Community Development Division in Thamesdown, for example, was sometimes seen 'as a bunch of left-wing activists stirring up communities, creating problems and unnecessary work'. That this reputation may be justified is suggested by the comment of one senior community worker in Newcastle, who wrote that 'community work if properly done will always create a certain amount of conflict, and does have a preoccupation with infuriating bureaucrats, almost as a hobby'. This disposition is related to the fact that, as a report from Peterborough notes, 'it is sometimes difficult to establish a workable relationship with the community when the professional is seen to be part of the Town Hall establishment'. For the community worker's credibility derives less from the local authority which employs him or her than from the neighbourhood groups whose members he is employed to help. This involves his being actively engaged in working with, and building up confidence among these groups and often encouraging them to make active representations to the local authority, which is also his employer and paymaster.

The strains which this conflict of roles provoke are now increasingly recognised and accepted by many local authorities which support this kind of work. Warrington, for example, notes that community development work can be

a stressful occupation. Long and unsocial hours, little obvious and quick returns for the workers' labour, dealing with conflict situations, can all lead to a feeling of isolation . . . Past experience has shown that the development of community consciousness and activity can lead to conflict within the community and with agencies servicing the community.

But this, it rightly adds, is often 'an inevitable part of a process which aims to encourage people to take a greater responsibility for their own affairs'. Tameside also recognises that 'tensions' and 'conflicts' will arise in a process in which local communities are actively encouraged to take part with the council in setting priorities and allocating resources for community education. And Islington expressly states that helping the public to 'take up issues about which they feel strongly . . . can bring community workers into conflict with their employers, the council itself. The council recognises that community workers must be free to do this'.

That this freedom can be misused is hardly surprising. A recent account of community work in Camden observes that most community work agencies had 'broad and often very generalised policies and in determining community work priorities and action all workers seem to have a considerable amount of autonomy'. The individual workers largely determine the work that they do and it is they who mainly choose what to put forward and what not to put forward to their managements for new work and future policies. As well as this high degree of operational autonomy, community workers are generally concerned to redress the balance of advantage in an unequal society by working particularly with ethnic minorities and other disadvantaged groups. This combination of a relatively high degree of professional autonomy with strong political beliefs can lead to difficulties if the community worker's political commitment is not balanced by an equally strong political sensitivity which can accurately assess what stances might or might not be acceptable in authorities of different political persuasions. Whereas many authorities would find unemployed centres totally acceptable, in Arun concern was expressed 'that such centres are underused by the unemployed and tend to become quasi political centres involved in the politics of unemployment'. Scunthorpe also noted that, paramount among the 'negative aspects which could arise from active community participation', was 'the use of the community centre as a political platform by unscrupulous members and associates'. In Newcastle, again, community workers employed by the local authority may sometimes have usurped their position and manipulated their communities by campaigning on general issues, like racism and equal opportunities, 'which the people in deprived neighbourhoods themselves did not regard as particularly important and for which councillors would have been reluctant to provide additional resources'.

Nor is this concern for the politicisation of community development confined to over-sensitive councillors and officers. For in nine out of the eleven ward meetings about decentralising services in Hounslow, concern was expressed about the danger that community councils, once established, would be politicised. People feared, on the one hand, that they would simply introduce party politics at local level, with voting along party lines and, on the other, that they would be dominated by local groups, such as tenants' associations. These associations were regarded as unrepresentative, undemocratic and sometimes as 'extreme'; and it was feared that they could easily come to dominate, and thus abuse the representative nature of these proposed councils.

Indeed, this anxiety about small and unrepresentative groups gaining undue influence in local councils was fairly general. Tameside, for example, notes that the proposed community education forums 'may become weak, ill attended and unproductive or they may become dominated by unrepresentative voices which disregard overall Council policies and/or the wide range of local needs and viewpoints'. Speaking of the residents' councils in Northampton, the liaision officer states that the councils are well aware of the 'pitfalls of "clique" formation' and that 'unrepresentative cliques have momentarily appeared in the past'. Scunthorpe again, notes that

paradoxically, the minority that have been charged to represent the interests of the majority at committee level are often prone to highlight certain deficiencies peculiar to their own philosophy and needs and even when claiming to represent the interests of a certain group of users are unlikely to represent the best interests of the organisation as a whole.

This tendency to unrepresentativeness grows from the fact that people do not necessarily wish to participate in local democratic institutions; and it is fallacious to suppose that they do. The Northampton report was right in stating that 'although it was felt that people should be "strongly encouraged" to participate . . . many would show no interest whatsoever'. Many people 'would feel naturally suspicious of any new initiative which seemed to be off-loading problems and responsibilities without giving any resources in return'. In Harlow, it was recognised that 'it is unlikely that people will come forward spontaneously to take part in the new structures immediately they are set up'. Southwark also commented that 'community involvement is still restricted to a relatively small number of people. In many cases it is only the politically and physically active, the articulate and the financially interested who take part.' Islington appreciated that it would require effort 'to draw in people [to community forums] who have not been used to expressing their views in this way'. It is therefore reasonable that efforts should be made to ensure that community groups are genuinely representative.

Conclusion
Clearly, a balance has to be struck between local interests and

priorities and the wider interests with which a local authority also has to be concerned. Councils have sometimes justified ignoring local groups' representations by arguing that their interests are 'sectional' and, as such, are automatically opposed to the general interest. This is a fallacious distinction. For the general interest is itself in part composed of lesser, special interests which contribute beneficially to that general interest. A voluntary organisation caring for the elderly is concerned with a sectional interest: but it is consistent with a local authority's more general interest in caring for those unable to care for themselves. What a local authority should rightly guard against is a sectional interest claiming more than it is reasonably entitled to claim, as against other interests and other claims which ought also to be supported. Furthermore, it must also balance the legitimate expectation that the autonomy of voluntary bodies and community groups will be respected with the local authority's equally proper concern that in its conduct, no less than the allocation of its funds, it should be subject to public accountability. Every local authority has it in its power to define the terms on which it relates to, and supports voluntary and community organisations. It is in the voluntary sector's interest, quite as much as the local authority's, that these terms should be both sympathetic and unambiguous.

How the relationship between local authorities and the voluntary sector will work out in the next five to ten years is unclear. Even in August 1988, the director of CIPFA argued that, by the end of the century, local government could be transformed from being the provider of everyday services to a much smaller agency whose function is to tackle the problems that the market mechanism cannot handle, with government grants being paid only for specific purposes. It could well be that the impending changes in local government, and especially the introduction of the poll-tax in 1990, will make it increasingly difficult to sustain a sympathetic and unambiguous relationship with the voluntary sector; and that the initiatives which we have described in this account will be jeopardised, if they are not entirely destroyed.

Such an outcome must be strongly resisted. These initiatives are extremely valuable. In general, they have succeeded in improving the services which the local authorities provide while at the same time increasing the scope of democratic citizenship. From simply providing community centres, for example, local authorities have been increasingly interested in encouraging the users to form associations to manage them. Similar moves towards associating the consumer more effectively with the delivery of services have led to the setting up of a variety of link organisations, such as education forums, residents' councils and community forums, as well as less formal means of doing so. Perhaps the most interesting proposition that we have recorded is that decentralising services requires greater local democracy.

Democracy, however, implies much more than people participating at the local authority's behest. It implies that they have the power to initiate ideas and local services themselves. In the support that has traditionally been given to local development agencies like rural community councils and councils for voluntary service, to voluntary services such as those provided by Relate and Gingerbread and increasingly in recent years to community groups, this principle of democratic pluralism is being vindicated. In these various ways, then, local authorities, such as those whose work has been described in this book, have been improving their services by relating their consumers more closely with their delivery. They have also been encouraging local democracy by supporting an independent voluntary sector and by promoting, through community development, a process of community education.

The danger which now faces both local government and the voluntary sector is that they will both forfeit such independence as they still retain and become merely parts of the apparatus of an increasingly centralised State. This would not only invalidate the community partnerships which have been developed so successfully in many parts of the country; it would also jeopardise the crucial principle of democratic pluralism to which those partnerships have given such tangible expression. That, in the end, is why they are so important and why they should be defended. It is that common interest which the Coalition, representing an important segment of the voluntary sector, shares with the local authorities which justifies its having taken the initiative to prepare this account of the local authorities' role in community development. We conclude it in the hope that it will help to promote that common concern in the anxious time which we both now face.

Sources

The following list includes the books and documents that have been used in preparing this study. Material which relates to a specific local authority is listed under that authority.

General

T. Aldous, 'Schools as a Resource', *Architects' Journal*, 21 November 1984.

D. Cliffe, *Community Work in Leicester*, CMCR, University of Leicester, 1985.

D. Donnison and P. Soto, *The Good City*, Heinemann, 1980.

David Francis, Paul Henderson, and David N. Thomas, *A Survey of Community Workers in the United Kingdom*, National Institute for Social Work, 1984.

B. Jordan, 'The Use of the Community Programme' in *Health and Social Care*, National Council for Voluntary Organisations, 1987.

J. Smith, *Public Involvement in Local Government: a Survey in England and Wales*, Community Projects Foundation, 1985.

John Spencer, *Stress and Release in an Urban Estate*, Tavistock Publications, 1964.

Peter Willmott with David Thomas, *Community in Social Policy*, Policy Studies Institute, September 1984.

Camden Community Work, Community Work Forum, Voluntary Action, Camden, April 1985.

Community Development – an AMA Policy Guidelines and Discussion Paper, Association of Metropolitan Authorities, [1988]

The Future of Voluntary Organisations, Croom Helm, 1977.

Joint Action – the Way Forward, Bedford Square Press, 1984.

Leisure Policy Now, Association of Metropolitan Authorities, [1986].

What Future for Local Government?, Institute of Economic Affairs, 1988.
Working Statement on Community Development, Standing Conference on Community Development, [1988].

Local authority sources
Arun District Council
  Arun District Council – the Next Four Years: Aims and Strategies Paper, May 1983.
  Community Support – a Review of Needs and Options for Action, February, 1984.
Birmingham City Council
  A Community Enterprise and Small Business Strategy, Economic Development Unit, 1986.
Blackburn Borough Council
  Review of Community Services, Community and Leisure Services Committee, 14 October 1987.
Cambridge City Council
  Community Welfare and Development Plan, 1985.
Cambridgeshire County Council
  The Way Ahead: Proposals for a County Strategy for Community Education, Community Education Review Steering Committee, May 1986.
  The Community's Education: Policy for Community Education in Cambridgeshire, 1987.
  Medium Term Planning 1988–1991 Guidelines, 1987.
  Proposals for Reorganising the Social Services Department, 1987.
  Cambridgeshire Villages, a Guide to Local Facilities, Cambridgeshire Community Council, 1985.
Cleveland County Council
  Neighbourhood Work in Grove Hill and Morton Grove, three annual reports, Research and Intelligence, Dec. 1984, Nov. 1985 and Dec. 1986.
Crewe and Nantwich District Council
  A.E.W. Body, *Cheshire: the County Handbook*, 1957.
  H.B. Rodgers, *South-Central Cheshire: An Analysis of Economic and Social Geography in Relation to Local Government Reorganisation*, University of Keele, 1980.
  Revised Management Structure, 1985.
  Proposed Divisional Structure for the Community Services Department, 1986.

Current Facts and Figures, Cheshire County Council, 1986.
Economic Development Policy Review – Discussion paper, 1987.
Guide to the Preparation of a Borough Recreation Plan (Draft), 1987.
The Recreation Division, Facilities and Structure, a paper prepared for Personnel Committee Visit, 1987.
Guide to the Preparation of a Borough Recreation Plan, 1987.
Report to the Community Services Committee: Grants to Parish Councils, Village Halls and Playing Fields, Adult Sports Organisations and Cultural Societies, 1987.
Overview: Recreation and Leisure Provision, 1987.
Dacorum Borough Council
Community Services Review, Leisure Services, [1984].
Review of Leisure 1985/1986, Leisure Services, 1986.
Ealing London Borough
Community Development and Consultation, Community Action Policy Group, 16 December 1987.
East Staffordshire District Council
Provision of Community Facilities, a report of the Chief Executive and Secretary, n.d.
Halton Borough Council
Richard Stevens, *Building Better Links: A Study of Services and Communications between a Local Council and the Public*, 1983.
Hampshire County Council
Hampshire Community Care Groups, Social Services Committee, 11 April 1986.
Review of Grants to Voluntary Organisations, memorandum from the Director of Social Services, 6 August 1986.
A Changing Role, Hampshire Community Care Groups Co-ordinating Committee, 12 June 1987.
Harlow Council
Draft Report of the Decentralisation and Democratisation Working Party, Resources and Policy Co-ordination Committee, [1986].
Neighbourhood Development, Policy and Planning Division, [1987].
Hereford and Worcester County Council
Where Now? Rural Community Development Project, September 1981.
First Annual Report, Community Development Unit, January 1985.

London Borough of Hounslow
  Community Associations, Policy Consultation Group, 8 September 1986.
  Notes on Public Meetings on Decentralisation, 1987.
Hull City Council
  Strategy for the Provision of Community Facilities in Kingston upon Hull: Community Centres, 17 January 1984.
Humberside County Council
  A Review of Adult Education: Interim Report, Education Department, January 1987.
Islington Council
  Going Local: Decentralisation in Practice, [1987].
Kirklees Metropolitan Council
  Community Work Team – Restructuring, Recreation and Amenities Committee, 21 July 1986.
Leeds City Council
  Report on Residents Consultations held June-October, 1985, Belle Isle North Priority Estates Project, Department of Housing, [1986].
Lincolnshire County Council
  Councils for Voluntary Service, Social Services Committee, 5 June 1986.
City of Newcastle upon Tyne
  Social Priority Areas and the Corporate Plan, a paper by Councillor Beecham, [1974].
  Scotswood Community Project Responsibility Document, Social Services Department, n.d.
  Priority Areas Project – Interim Report, Performance and Review Sub-Committee, 26 February 1981.
  Background Information on Newcastle's Priority Areas Project, Chief Executive's Office, [1981].
  Newcastle upon Tyne – 'City Profiles': Results from the 1981 Census, Policy Services, 1983.
  Community Work in Newcastle, report by Joint Officer Group to the Youth and Community Recreation Services Sub-Committee, 16 April 1986.
  An Introduction to Newcastle City Council, [1986].
  Grant Programme 1987/88, Social Services Policy Sub-Committee, 2 February 1987.
New Forest District Council
  Looking Ahead at Leisure in the New Forest District, [1987].

Northampton Borough Council
B. P. Gibson, *Ten Years of Residents: The Eyes and Ears of the Community*, [1987].
Northumberland County Council
Community Education: Report of Youth and Adult Education Service, Further and Adult Education Sub-Committee, 5 November 1985.
Nottinghamshire County Council
Community Development Work, Social Services Committee, 29 January 1985.
Peterborough City Council
Community Development – Future Policy, Leisure and Amenities Committee, 18 November 1985.
Scunthorpe Borough Council
A Comparative Analysis of Community Centre Provision, Leisure and Recreation Department, March 1982.
Slough Borough Council
Leisure Strategy: Completing the Picture, April 1986.
London Borough of Southwark
Eric Adams, *Community Development and Local Government: London Borough of Southwark*, NCN, July 1987.
Stevenage Borough Council
Stephen Humble, *Community Development and Local Government: the Case of Stevenage Borough Council*, NCN, 1987.
Tameside Metropolitan Borough
Community Education and Development in Tameside, Report of the Community Education Review Group, August 1986.
Thamesdown Borough Council
Maurice Broady, *The Statutory Authority and Voluntary Social Welfare*, a report to Thamesdown Borough Council, December 1982.
M. Harloe, *Swindon, a Town in Transition*, Heinemann, 1975.
Gorse Hill: a Community Profile, Community Planning Committee, 15 March 1984.
Paul Curphey and Rod Grant, *Having a Say: The Swindon Under-25s Survey*.
Thamesdown International Youth Co-ordinating Committee, 1984.
An Area Profile of Eldene and Liden, Community Planning Committee, 23 May 1985.
A New Vision for Thamesdown: Strategy Statement, 1985.

Home Economic Activity and the Built Environment, report of a seminar, 3 December 1985.

Walcot East: a Community Profile, Community Planning Committee, 1 September 1986.

In a Cold Climate: Meeting the Needs of Ethnic Minority Elderly People in Thamesdown, report of a conference, 25 November 1986.

Grants to Voluntary Bodies 1987–88, Community Planning Committee, 2 February 1987.

The Effects of the Rail Works Redundancies upon Communities in Thamesdown, 1987.

Warrington Borough Council

Community Development and the Proposed Expansion of the Community Action Areas Project, Report of the Acting Planning and Estates Officer to the Policy and Resources Committee, 5 January 1987.

Index